PASSOVER

SURVIVAL KIT

"The Survival Kit can help make Passover an acquisition, not just a memory."

Rabbi Yaacov Weinberg – Baltimore
Rosh Yeshiva, Ner Israel Rabbinical College

"Apisdorf understands the heartbeat of our generation with incomparable clarity; he knows where it hurts and what to do about it. The Survival Kit will help thousands turn Passover the nightmare into Pesach the dream."

Rabbi Michel and Rebbitzen Feige Twerski – Milwaukee
Congregation Beth Jehudah

"Good news! Another ground-breaking book from Shimon Apisdorf. His genius will undoubtedly transform Passover for all who study this remarkable manual."

Rabbi Ephraim Z. Buchwald – New York
Director, National Jewish Outreach Program

PASSOVER SURVIVAL KIT

by

Shimon Apisdorf

published by

66 North Merkle Road, Columbus, Ohio 43209

(614) 338-0774

ISBN 1-881927-01-6

Cover Illustration by Julius Ciss

Spine Logo by E.R. Design

PRINTED IN THE UNITED STATES OF AMERICA

Group Sales: The *Passover Survival Kit, Survival Kit Haggadah,* and *Rosh Hashanah Yom Kippur Survival Kit* are available to schools, synagogues and community organizations by special order. See page 158.

ACKNOWLEDGMENTS

Donna Cohen, Amy Schildhouse, Helen and Joe Berman, Blair Axel, William Schottenstein, Jake Koval, Dov Friedberg, Michael Hart, Rick Cohen, Eric Schramm, Josh Greenberg, Terry Sankey, Kim McGarvey, Rabby Aryeh Kaltman, Daniel Libicki, Mr. Michael Seidemann, Rabbi Jonathan Rosenberg, Rabbi Asher Resnick, Rabbi Yaacov Weinberg *shlita*, Harry Apisdorf, the Tree of D., and EMETT.

APPRECIATION

Congregation Ahavas Sholom, a spiritual home. Sherri Cohen, dedicated typist. Russell Simmons, a humble hero. Ann Apisdorf, Assistant Director of Marketing. Rabbi Noah Weinberg, Rosh Hayeshiva and source of inspiration.

SPECIAL THANKS

Mr. and Mrs. David and Bernice Apisdorf. Parents, friends, teachers, role models and full-time cheering section.

Mr. and Mrs. Robert and Charlotte Rothenburg. Examples of kindness, generosity and deep sincerity.

Esther Rivka, Ditzah Leah, Yitzchak Ben Zion. Every day with you is a prayer answered and a dream fulfilled.

Miriam. You have given new meaning to the words love, life and laughter. Your patience, hands-on dedication and *bitachon* are woven into every line of this book.

Hakadosh Baruch Hu, source of all blessing.

CONTENTS

THE SURVIVAL KIT HAGGADAH

PASSOVER
SURVIVAL KIT

1

INTRODUCTION

I

It is very easy for me to say the words *I love you* to my wife, and that's a problem.

These words deserve to be uttered with the deepest of feelings — with a keen awareness of their impact and implications, and with a sense of awe. The intimacy of a husband and wife bonded in love is something transcendent and sanctified. And *I love you* is so inadequate. Not only does one challenge the laws of nature by attempting to capture *love* in words; but to make matters even worse, these are words that have been subjected to endless abuse and dragged through every gutter of inappropriate context and insincerity. We love our cars, our dogs, and our favorite TV shows. If we can love anything, then perhaps the word *love* has come to mean nothing at all.

Imagine the intensity of the words *I love you*, if they were spoken only when human beings desired to express their most cherished feelings of closeness, caring, and admiration. I believe that life as we know it would be substantially different.

This dilemma of working with expressions which have been used to death is one I am now grappling with. In search of words adequate enough to welcome you to the *Passover Survival Kit*, I am frozen somewhere between feelings and written expression. There is something I want to say, but at every turn I am faced by the demons of triteness and cliché. Emotions are hemmed in by a maze of hollow-sounding standards like *thank you* and *I feel so fortunate*.

But Passover is approaching, the printer won't wait, and silence is an insufferable option. So here we go:

> *I feel that my life has been blessed. I am grateful for the many gifts I am aware of, and also for those of which I remain unaware. I had the good fortune of being raised with a love for my Jewishness. Though why I loved it, I wasn't quite sure. One blessing led to another and eventually I spent six years living around the corner from the Western Wall. Even more years were invested exploring the identity I had been raised to cherish. I met my bride in Jerusalem. She molds our lives around the principle of growth, our children are sweet, and the Yom Tovim — the holidays — in our home are amongst the most precious moments we share. And now, in some small way, we would like to share our Passover with you.*

II

As the world gets smaller and smaller, our experiential framework begins to look more and more alike. We place a call from an office in Hong Kong and use a card to access our phone messages in Houston. Could we not just as easily be placing that call from London, Montreal, or Battle Creek, Michigan? While this homogenization of life casts an umbral pall over the faces of men, it also works to create new commonalities and points of departure for communication within our species. As such, though we don't yet know one another, I sense that there is a good deal we share. And so I offer you the *Passover Survival Kit*.

Few of the ideas contained in this book are genuinely novel. They are a bit of the Judaism I have thus far learned, refracted through the lens of this American Jew's attempt to live a contemplative Jewish life.

I thank the Almighty, who has authored for me a life of blessing. And I thank my wife, Miriam, who has begun to skillfully edit that life so as to free its potential for expressing those blessings.

In the end, that is what this book is all about: freedom. The freedom to grasp our potential as people, and as a Jewish people. To harness that potential and to creatively direct it towards a fulfillment of our inner most aspirations. Passover is not only the anniversary of our exodus, it is a spiritual rendezvous with freedom. The holiday is a guide, the Seder and the Haggadah a map, and together it is all a fabulous opportunity and adventure.

And finally I thank you, for caring enough to pick up this slender volume, and for allowing me to share its collection of thoughts, ideas, and feelings. And I ask you, please, be kind enough to share our legacy with someone you love.

Chag Kasher V'sameach
Happy Passover

Shimon Apisdorf

2

SURVIVAL KIT USER'S GUIDE

The purpose of the Passover Survival Kit is to make this holiday, and the Seder in particular, an experience which is thoroughly relevant to some of the most important issues in your life. This book will serve as a friendly gateway through which you will enter the world of Passover and see it as you have never seen it before. Like inanimate objects magically brought to life by Disney, the *Survival Kit* will introduce you to the fixtures of Passover while revealing that each possesses a lively inner life that is just waiting to speak with you. Once inside this new dimension, you will discover that the observances, customs, *mitzvot* (commandments), prayers and the Haggadah itself have all exchanged their drab ritualistic personas for the casual attire of an old friend. Having stopped by for a late night cup of coffee you will end up spending hours talking about matters which are deeply important to you. The thoughtful moments slip by and suddenly it is time to part. A smile of fulfilled contentment tinged with sadness flutters across your lips as you say goodnight. You vow to speak again soon.

Such is the potential of a thoughtful Seder experience. Here are a few suggestions that will help you get the most out of this book, and this holiday.

I.   **Before the Seder:** Jewish law designates the thirty days prior to Passover as a preparatory period for the upcoming holiday.

   A.   Set aside ten minutes a day during the month before Passover to read through the *Survival Kit*.
   B.   Read chapter 6 (The Passover Puzzle), and think about one idea which you will want to focus on at each point in the Seder. Jot this idea down at the appropriate place in your Haggadah to serve as a reminder at the Seder.
   C.   On you own, or with your family, read the Haggadah section of this book. This will give everyone a sense of the potential inherent in the experience you are about to share. When doing this, you may want to have other Haggadahs on hand which contain commentary and explanations. These resources will help answer questions which may arise that are not addressed by the *Survival Kit.*

II. **During the Seder:**

   A.   Before you carry out any of the observances at the Seder, i.e., drinking wine or eating matzah, take a moment to read about the meaning of that action.
      i.   Always ask yourself: What is the meaning of the action I am now performing, and how does it relate to my life?

ii. When contemplating the meaning of your actions, ask: if this is what Passover is about, what does that tell me about Judaism?

B. Don't be afraid of being a straggler. If there is a portion of the Seder which touches you, which speaks to you with particular relevance, then stay there for a while. Mull the thoughts over in your mind, and give them a moment to sink in. You will always be able to catch up, and if you see you may have to start eating a few minutes after everyone else, that's okay — just politely ask that they save you some brisket.

3

MORE THAN FOUR: TWELVE QUESTIONS PEOPLE ASK ABOUT PASSOVER

(I)

Question: Why is the Passover dinner called a "Seder"?

Answer: The Hebrew word *seder* means order, or arrangement. The Passover Seder is comprised of fifteen sequential steps, and thus it is quite fitting that the word *seder* is used to portray the gist of the evening's proceedings. (For more on the meaning of each of these fifteen parts of the Seder, see chapter 6, The Passover Puzzle on page 55.)

Insight: Shortcuts are convenient. They save time, effort, and sometimes even money. They can also be quite illusory. Sure, you can figure out an ingenious back-alley route to sneak by rush-hour traffic or curl up with a single volume containing three-page summaries of everything from Shakespeare to Fulghum, but don't try it in life. Not with your children, not with your spouse, and certainly not with yourself.

If you want self-awareness, personal growth, deeper relationships, and a life of integrity — sorry, no shortcuts allowed. Only *seder*, only order will do. Deeper living just doesn't flourish in the land of quick fixes. No child ever reaches adulthood without paying a visit to adolescence and no adult achieves inner maturation without first embarking on an orderly, if daring, course of human development.

(II)

Question: Why do we read the Haggadah on Passover?

Answer: The holiday of Passover marks the anniversary of the birth of the Jewish nation. The story of the Jewish nation is one of individuals who became a family who became a people. The great individuals who laid the spiritual foundation of Jewish peoplehood were Abraham and Sarah, their son and daughter-in-law Isaac and Rebecca, and their son and daughters-in-law Jacob, Rachel, and Leah. From Jacob, Rachel, and Leah came a family of seventy people who, due to a famine in Israel, were forced to migrate to Egypt. In Egypt this family grew and prospered to such an extent that they eventually came to be seen as a threat by their Egyptian hosts. Respect and admiration turned to contempt, and finally to an organized program of enslavement and oppression. After 210 years, a series of unheeded warnings by Moses to Pharaoh, and ten plagues, G-d liberated a nation which had grown from the original family of seventy people. The exodus from Egypt marks the birth of the Jewish people. Seven weeks later this newly conceived nation received the Torah at Mount Sinai.

The Haggadah is the story of the birth of the Jews as a people. It deals primarily with the events in Egypt which led from slavery to liberation, though it also spans the entire period from Abraham to the giving of the Torah at Mount Sinai. One could say that the

Haggadah is our national birth certificate as well as our Declaration of Independence. More than just a historical document, it also speaks of the ideals and values which constitute the essence of our national consciousness and identity.

HISTORICAL OVERVIEW

Haggadah

Abraham and Sarah — 2080/1671 BCE

Isaac and Rebecca — 2110/1641 BCE

Jacob and Rachel and Leah — 2180/1561 BCE

Jacob's family migrates to Egypt — 2238/1496 BCE

Period of enslavement begins— 2331/1430 BCE

Exodus from Egypt — 2448/1313 BCE

Torah given at Mount Sinai — 2448/1313 BCE

Post-Haggadah

The Jewish people enter the land of Israel — 2489/1272 BCE

First Temple destroyed by the Babylonians — 3338/423 BCE

Second Temple destroyed by the Romans — 3830/70 CE

Jewish communities develop around the world — 3338/423 BCE– Present

Birth of modern Israel — 5708/1948 CE

Jews celebrate Passover in Boston, Buenos Aires,
     and Bangkok — 5755/1994 CE

Next Year in Jerusalem

Insight: The word *haggadah* means to tell, or to relate. The Haggadah is a vivid narrative which is set in the context of a parent-child dialogue. Passover, with the Haggadah as its focus, tells every Jew three things: who you are, where you came from, and what you stand for. The message inherent in the Haggadah is that Jewish identity and continuity hinge on encouraging children to ask questions and being prepared as parents to provide sensitive and substantive answers. In Judaism, being learned, knowledgeable, and wise is not only a goal, it's a prerequisite.

(III)

Question: Why do people spend so much time cleaning their homes before Passover?

Answer: Though homespun historians point to the practicality of this ritualized version of spring cleaning, the fact is that cleaning one's home is an integral part of Passover. The Torah teaches that no Jew may eat, own, or even have in his or her possession any type of baked or leavened grain products during the week of Passover. In response to this commandment, Jews throughout the millennia have worked to ensure that their homes are 100 percent leaven-free for Passover. To achieve this, entire families embark upon a thorough house cleaning which culminates in *bedikat chometz*, the search for leaven on the night before Passover. Meticulous extirpation of every last crumb from otherwise innocent-looking nooks and crannies inevitably involves considerable work and results in a degree of cleanliness which is second to none.

Insight: The prototypical form of forbidden leaven is bread. Matzah, the alter-ego of bread, is simply dough that was never allowed to ferment and rise. The most obvious difference between bread and matzah is also the most striking: one is flat while the other is all puffed up.

As a rule, Judaism encourages all attempts at personal growth and meaningful accomplishment. However, the Torah is leery of our becoming carried away by pride in our achievements. On Passover, bread comes to represent the big headed swagger of arrogance. For one week a year we rid ourselves of all traces of breadlike products in an effort to detach our consciousness from the grips of an over-inflated ego. This enables us to reestablish a balanced picture of who we are, who we aren't, and who we truly want to be.

(IV)

Question: Why is this night different from all other nights?

Answer: To understand the essence of what makes Passover so distinctive one must understand the Jewish concept of holidays in general. The meaning of Jewish holidays goes beyond the historical events which provide their contextual backdrop. Every holiday possesses a central message for all Jews, and each has its own thematic personality through which this message is communicated. For example, the holiday of Sukkot is "a time of joy," while the Ninth of *Av* is a time of mourning. With the observance of each holiday these respective themes are studied, reflected upon, and more fully integrated into our personalities.

It is in this sense that Passover is known as the "*time of freedom.*" More than physical freedom from bondage, Passover is about the nature of human freedom; a quality of freedom which is neither superfluous in a land of democratic liberties nor cynical under a dictatorial regime.

Insight: Every Jewish holiday is a window of opportunity for growth. The golden opportunity of Passover is to understand and achieve new dimensions in freedom. When observance of the various *mitzvot* and laws converge in an atmosphere of thoughtful study and reflection, a metamorphic process is set into motion. With time, year after year, what had become an overly ritualized family reunion can be transformed into a fountainhead of insight and inspiration.

(V)

Question: What is the significance of the Seder plate?

Answer: The Seder plate is comprised of ten different elements. Three whole matzahs, a roasted bone, an egg, bitter herbs, charoset (chopped almonds, apple, cinnamon, and wine), a vegetable (karpas), chazeret, (a second portion of bitter herb or vegetable), and lastly, the Seder plate itself.

Passover, the original multimedia experience, presents us with a dazzling array of objects and images, each of which direct our thoughts and feelings towards another nuance of the potential contained within the entire Seder experience. Each of the ten Seder plate items is a touchstone which steers our attention towards a deeper understanding of Passover, of being Jewish, and of ourselves.

Insight: The following are brief explanations of the items which make up the Seder plate:

1. **Three matzahs** — The Jewish people are divided into three subgroups: *Kohein*, describing the spiritual leaders who were responsible for the daily activities in the Temple; *Levi*, who assisted the *Kohein* and bore a particular responsibility for the teaching of Torah to the people; and *Israel*, who constitute the great majority of the Jewish nation. Today, every Jew is descended from one of these three groups.

Each piece of matzah represents one of these groups, with the underlying message being one of diversity in unity. Though we may have various talents, functions, and areas of specialization, we must ultimately be united around the banner of achieving the common goals of the Jewish people.

2. **The roasted bone** — When the Temple stood in Jerusalem, every family purchased a lamb known as the "Passover Offering." It was an obligation for all individuals and families to travel to Jerusalem for the holiday of Passover, where the lamb would be eaten as part of the Seder meal. Today, in the absence of the Temple, the roasted bone serves as a reminder of that Passover lamb.

Lambs steadily follow their shepherd. So, too, the Jewish people. While others latch onto men, machines, and social movements to lead them through life, the Jewish people have always insisted that above all, it is G-d's lead we are striving to follow.

3. **The egg** — In addition to the Passover lamb, there was a second offering. This offering, the *chagigah*, or Festival Offering, was a more generic offering that was also brought to the Temple for other holidays. On Passover it served as the main course at the Seder meal.

The egg is used as the symbol of choice for the Festival Offering because eggs are both readily accessible and easy to cook. In this, they are like all Jewish holidays, requiring dedicated preparation, and possessing a potential for growth that is both accessible to everyone and which requires no expertise to be realized.

4. **Bitter herbs** — On a physical plane, the bitter herbs recall the anguish of our slavery in Egypt. On another level, this bitterness is one born of the strife we experience when the trappings of life seem to commit us to a direction not of our own making. (For more on bitter herbs, see page 69.)

5. **Charoset** — This pasty substance is reminiscent of the mortar used by Jewish slaves to make bricks in Egypt. It is a favorite of kids of all ages, and a large part of its function is simply to arouse the curiosity of children. They will be stimulated to ask questions like, "what is this?" and "why do we eat it?" and in so doing, they open a door through which parents can engage their children in discussion about the Seder, Passover, the symbols, their meanings, and all the rest.

Cinnamon, which used to come in sticks before it came in neatly packaged plastic shakers, recalls the straw which was mixed into the mortar. The wine is the innocent blood of Jewish slaves who perished under the weight of oppression. While these elements remind us of the harsh circumstances of our slavery, there is also hope and heroism mixed into the charoset.

The Hebrew word for almonds, *shekadim*, is derived from a root meaning "hasty". Though the period of slavery in Egypt could have easily stretched on for generations, in the end G-d hastened our redemption. (For more on this, see pages 109-111) Today we also hope for the early return of a unified people to the land of Israel.

The apples are a reminder of the heroines of Passover, the fearless Jewish women. Our sages teach that in a world darkened by oppressive slavery, horrific degradation, and Pharaoh's decree to kill all firstborn male babies, Jewish men despaired of future salvation. Jewish women, on the other hand, never lost hope. They insisted on having children even when their husbands questioned the rationality of bringing children into a world of misery. Our sages teach that Jewish women would hide in the apple orchards to secretly give birth. Where others saw only darkness, the Jewish women saw the possibility for a brighter future. They believed, they were committed, and they simply wouldn't buckle. In other words — they were free. In the words of the Talmud, *"The Jewish people were redeemed in the merit of the righteous women, and the future redemption will also be in their merit."*

6. **Karpas**, the piece of vegetable — In ancient times vegetables were served as appetizers at the finest meals and banquets. On the night of Passover every Jew is a member of an aristocratic family. We are people of status and wealth, as free as a king in his palace. We grace our Seder plate with karpas, a venerable sign of opulence, to express our sense that the feeling of Jewishness is the feeling of nobility.

7. **Chazeret**, a second portion of bitter herb — During the Seder we eat bitter herbs twice: once by itself and once as a sandwich with matzah. (For more on this sandwich, see page 70).

8. The **Seder plate** itself — nothing that is required for the Seder is missing from the Seder plate. Again, like a royal banquet, nothing is lacking. Every commoner dreams of what a privileged life inside the palace would be like. We Jews are there; and we wouldn't trade being Jewish for anything in the world — would we?

(VI)

Question: Why do we hide the afikomen and give gifts to the children who find it?

Answer: In many ways children are the stars of the Seder night. Jewish law states that the Seder should begin as soon after nightfall as possible in order to insure the participation of children. Various customs, including spreading nuts on the table, exist specifically to arouse the curiosity of children and to stimulate their active involvement. Likewise, the hiding and seeking of the afikomen. The annual afikomen hunt has a way of transforming even the most bleary-eyed youngster into an exuberant Seder enthusiast.

Insight: Like a child on the trail of the afikomen, we too must see ourselves as seekers — seeking for truth and meaning, for the kind of fulfillment that lasts longer than a week, and for riches that transcend the material. And, like children in search of the afikomen, when focused on the urgency of our search, we will experience our efforts not only as the price of life but as its thrill and pleasure.

(VII)

Question: What is the Passover lamb?

Answer: When the Temple stood in Jerusalem, there were numerous types of sacrifices offered for various reasons and on different occasions.* One of the most prominent of all the sacrifices was the *Korban Pesach*, or Passover Offering. It is a *mitzvah* for every Jew to bring a Passover lamb to Jerusalem and to eat a piece of it at the Seder. In practice, entire families and often groups of families would share one lamb.

The roots of this *mitzvah* are found in the Torah at the time of the exodus. Four days before leaving Egypt, every Jewish family

---

*The Hebrew word for sacrifice is *korban*, which comes from the verb meaning *to draw close*. Judaism never saw sacrifices as gifts to either appease or please G-d. Rather they were spiritual mechanisms which served to intensify the feeling of closeness between man and G-d. For more on the meaning of sacrifices, see the *Rosh Hashanah Yom Kippur Survival Kit*, p. 94-97.

was commanded to take a chief Egyptian god — the lamb — and tie it up in their homes. Then, in the waning moments of bondage, each family slaughtered this revered diety and daubed its blood on the doorpost of their homes. That night, when the Egyptians were struck by the tenth plague — the death of the firstborn son — it was this blood which distinguished Jewish homes from Egyptian homes.

Insight: The Hebrew word *pesach* means to skip, or pass over. Both the name of the holiday — Passover — and the name of its special offering — the Passover sacrifice — are derived from the seminal event of "skipping over" the Jewish homes. This act of "passing over" was a moment of subtle distinction. The Passover lamb was the vehicle for this distinction, and the concept of distinctions is endemic to Passover.

If Passover means to draw distinctions — to skip over one thing and opt for another — then a part of being Jewish is being able to discriminate: between right and wrong, between meaningful and trivial, and between spiritual and mundane. In an age of subjective spirituality and moral relativism, the prospect of drawing distinctions seems almost passé. But one thing we learned when slaughtering that first Egyptian god, is that freedom requires the courage to be slightly out of vogue.

(VIII)

Question: Do you have to read the whole Haggadah or can you skip the boring parts?

Answer: The reading of the entire Haggadah is the way in which one fulfills his or her obligation to speak about the exodus from Egypt on the night of Passover. In order to realize the full benefit of this *mitzvah*, one must both read and understand the complete text of the Haggadah. This means that if you don't understand Hebrew then you shouldn't read it in Hebrew. This also implies, that beyond understanding the words, you should strive to discern their deeper meanings and messages.

Insight: Look at it this way. Imagine that while rummaging through a long-neglected corner in your attic you were to find a dusty, handwritten manuscript authored by your great-grandfather. Wouldn't you be curious to see what he wrote? And what if the opening lines read, *"To my dear children, this is the most important book you will ever read. It is about Jewish life and the wisdom of living written by a Jew who dedicated his life to the pursuit of wisdom. Countless hours have been devoted to finding the words and the thoughts which I trust will serve as a faithful guide in life, and as a key to your freedom...."*

The yellowed pages of that manuscript are the timeless folios of every Haggadah. That great-grandfather is the collective wisdom of our greatest sages. You are the heir who happened upon those lost words, and the legacy of freedom is yours to discover.

(IX)

Question: Why do we drink four cups of wine at the Seder?

Answer: The enslavement of the Jewish people did not happen overnight. The Egyptians orchestrated a deliberate progression of events that lead from our being a highly respected minority to vilified outsiders and ultimately a subhuman slave caste.[*] Likewise, the redemption from bondage did not take place in one sudden flash. When the Torah describes the transition from slavery to freedom, it uses four different words to indicate four stages of transformation. These four words are known as "the four expressions of redemption." They are:

1. *V'hotzaiti* — "and I removed you"
2. *V'hitzalti*   — "and I rescued you"
3. *V'goalti*   — "and I redeemed you"
4. *V'lakachti* — "and I took you"

The four cups of wine correspond to these "four expressions of redemption."

---

[*] These events are described by the Torah in the book of Exodus, chapters 1:8 - 2:25. The translation and commentary by Rabbi Samson Raphael Hirsch provides an insightful look at this chain of events.

Insight: The effect of wine — good wine — is that it lifts your spirits and helps you feel good. In Judaism, *life* and *pleasure* are synonymous. And, though the trials of life may obscure the pleasure of life's blessings — still — life is a pleasure. Wine in Jewish life is never used to drown out pain, but rather to assist one in reconnecting to the feeling that life is pleasurable.

On Passover, the drinking of wine lifts us in two ways. (1) The redemption from Egypt took place a long time ago. Sometimes it is difficult to feel connected to these events and to the pleasure of being a part of the Jewish nation. Wine helps. (2) Though the attainment of freedom may be cause for dancing in the streets, it also carries with it the burden of responsibility. This looming weight of accountability — the nuts and bolts of sovereignty — is enough to temper any celebration. So we drink a little wine — to lift us, and to remind us that long after the headlines have faded, the deepest pleasure of freedom still remains. The pleasure of assuming the reins of responsibility. Of rolling up our sleeves and beginning to tackle the thankless tasks necessary to transform promise into substance and dreams into reality.

(X)

Question: What makes food products "Kosher for Passover"?

Answer: A 50 percent price increase.

Insight: The truth of the matter is that the business of ensuring that food products are truly Kosher for Passover is a highly skilled and technical field. It requires both advanced Jewish scholarship as well as a sophisticated knowledge of all facets of the food industry. There is more in our food than food, you know. There are also stabilizers, colors, artificial flavorings, additives, binders, preservatives, and even pieces of the kitchen sink!

The answer to the question, "What could possibly be wrong with a stick of butter?" is that it may well contain cultures and coloring agents derived from *chometz* (leavened grain products) or even lactic acid containing derivatives which are not permissible on Passover. And, while "coffee, is coffee, is coffee" may ring true, there happen to be manufacturers who use grain additives in their coffees or ethyl acetate — a derivative of *chometz* — in their decaffeination process. When one casts a doubting glance at a bottle of "pure" orange juice which has suddenly doubled in price, further investigation may show that bran is commonly used in the filtering of many fruit juices. So, while our Passover grocery bills seem a bit exorbitant, we must appreciate that behind every reputable "Kosher for Passover" label stands an army of highly skilled experts. And, thanks to them, our clockwork consumption of everything from cola to applesauce to potato chips is able to proceed smoothly throughout the entire week of Passover. Now that's what I call freedom.

(XI)

Question: Why do people sit on pillows and recline at the Seder?

Answer: Reclining at the Seder is an outward display of freedom. Royalty would often have special lounges upon which they would recline while eating their meals. On the night of the Seder we project the feeling that a Jewish life is a royal life.

Insight: Jewish law makes a point of saying that even a pauper is obligated to recline at the Seder. Often times people equate wealth with freedom, the assumption being; the wealthier I become, the freer I will be. To this, the pauper's reclining at the Seder retorts, it's not how much you have that determines your freedom, but what you do with what you have.

No matter how numerous or how meager your possessions, when they are used to help others, and to promote meaningful endeavors, then they are instruments of freedom. Conversely, when wealth becomes a means to amass a vast collection of self-indulgent toys, then each new acquisition becomes another set of designer handcuffs.

(XII)

Question: Why do we have a cup of wine at the Seder table called the cup of Elijah?

Answer: Elijah the Prophet occupies a fascinating place in Jewish historical consciousness. Our tradition teaches that as history approaches the climactic era of universal peace and brotherhood, it will be Elijah the Prophet who will announce the heralding of the messianic era. Additionally, when the sages in the Talmud were unable to definitively resolve certain questions of law or practice they would often state that they would just have to wait for Elijah. With the advent of the final era, one of Elijah's roles will be to resolve all those lingering scholarly quandaries.

There is an opinion in the Talmud which states that five cups of wine, not four, are to be drunk at the Seder. In practice we follow the majority opinion and drink only four cups. In deference to the minority opinion, however, we pour the fifth cup of wine even though no one drinks from it. This fifth cup of wine bears the name of Elijah because it is he who will eventually resolve this question, as well as many others.

Insight: Jews believe in questions. Whether it is the innocent question of a youngster at the Seder or the penetrating query of a Talmudic sage, Judaism neither hides its questions nor hides from them. Thoughtful questions fueled by a relentless pursuit of truth and wisdom are part and parcel of the Jewish experience. We celebrate questions and applaud a desire for truth that burns not for a day, a semester, or even for years — but until the end of time itself.

4

THE FREEDOM PAPERS:
FOUR DIMENSIONS OF FREEDOM

I
FREEDOM AND SELF-AWARENESS

"I can do anything in the world I want. There is just one problem — I don't know what I want."

Question: Is this person free?
Answer: Yes, and no.

Yes, she possesses the freedom to do whatever she wants, but then again no, for she is trapped by the stifling parameters of limited self-awareness. Though totally unrestrained to go any place at all, she is unable to take even the smallest step for lack of knowing where she wants to go.

*   *   *

"Sometimes I get so frustrated. I know exactly what I want, but I still can't seem to achieve my goals. Halfway through one project my motivation wanes and I'm on to something else. I get distracted, caught up in other things — I just can't seem to stay focused."

Question: Is this person free?

Answer: Yes, and no.

Yes, because he knows what he wants to accomplish and possesses the resources necessary for success, but then again no. For some reason he has become paralyzed by forces he seems unable to control. Is he afraid to take risks or is there an underlying lack of self-confidence? Is he still waiting for someone to take care of him or is he just plain lazy?

Yes, he is free, but unable to harness the inner strength to actualize his freedom; sadly, he is also a slave.

*   *   *

Now, let us look into the mirror of irony. The year is 1978 and the man's name is Yosef Mendelovich. The setting: a dank cell deep within the bowels of the Christopol prison in the Soviet Union. The date is April 12. On the Jewish calendar it is the 14th of *Nisan,* one day before the start of Passover.

Yosef is a prisoner. He is a gaunt human shell, and he is about to light a candle. Made of hoarded bits of string, pitiful droplets of oil, and stray slivers of wax, this is a candle fashioned by Yosef's own hands.

The candle is lit — the search for chometz begins.

Sometime earlier Yosef had complained of back problems. The infirmary in hell provided him with mustard to serve as a therapeutic plaster. Unused then, this mustard would later reappear as maror — bitter herbs — at Yosef's seder table. A long-saved onion bulb in water had produced a humble bit of greenery.

This would be his karpas. And the wine? Raisins were left to soak in an old jelly jar, water was occasionally added, and fermentation was prayed for. This was wine. The Haggadah which Yosef transcribed into a small notebook before being imprisoned had now been set to memory. The original was secretly passed on to another dangerous enemy of the State: Anatoly Sharansky.

Question: Is Yosef free?

Answer: Yes, and no.

No, he cannot do whatever he wants. He has been denied even the liberty to know when the sun shines and the stars twinkle. For Yosef the world of free men doesn't even begin to exist.

But then again, yes. Yosef, perhaps, is more free even than his captors. Clearly self-aware, he knows exactly who he is, what he wants, and is prepared to pay any price to have it. Today he walks the streets of Israel, studies Torah, and buys box after box of matzah to serve at his Seder. He is a free man now, just as he was even behind those lifeless prison walls.

*   *   *

Self-awareness means that we are able to stand outside of ourselves. In so doing we are able to look within and, to a degree, to assess our own inner workings. How do we react to people and situations, and why? When are we at ease, when are we tense, and when do we feel a sense of balance? What are our goals and priorities, and what are the values reflected in those goals? Are those values ours, or are they someone else's? Where are we strong and where do we need to grow? What comes naturally and what requires great effort? Who do we love, what is it we love in them, and are we able to express that love? Are we being honest with ourselves, with others, and with G-d? Are we headed in the right direction? If not — why not, and if yes, to what do we attribute our success?

Unaware of all these things, we remain mired in a dense fog of confusion and doubt. Can we ever be fully self-aware? Probably not. But aware enough to set ourselves free? Yes, and this is one of life's most pivotal challenges.

The achievement and maintenance of freedom is available only through the ongoing struggle for self-awareness. This process of clarification, coupled with the conviction to follow wherever it may lead, is the only way to achieve a spiritually sensitive, value-driven life of liberty. Ironically, this freedom can land you in a prison where you are the captor, while your guards are the prisoners. Just ask Yosef Mendelovich — one of the freest people who ever walked this earth.

II
IDEALISM, CHOMETZ, AND FREEDOM

Idealism: More Than Kid Stuff

One day I walked into the high school classroom where I teach and was nearly tackled by a wide-eyed teenager supercharged with excitement. She could barely contain herself: "Rabbi Apisdorf, Rabbi Apisdorf," she screeched, pleaded, and politely demanded, "I have to show you something!" Before I could even blink — much less respond — a newsletter from Amnesty International had been thrust to within an inch of my glasses.

April is a bright, energetic girl who is out to do no less than change the world she lives in. She is an adolescent mix of Mother Teresa and a rock-n-roll icon gyrating to benefit the latest victims of flooding in Bangladesh. And she means it.

A few weeks after my encounter with April's membership in Amnesty International, I was duely informed that she was now a card-carrying member of Green Peace. Before long she would be directing the school's Thanksgiving food drive, educating all who would listen about the plight of third-world babies, championing the cause of America's homeless, praying for an endangered species of rhinoceros, and graciously soliciting my sponsorship of bowling for AIDS. At ten cents a pin, I had no choice.

As time passed, her infectious zeal began to stir some long dormant feelings; memories of what it felt like to believe that the world truly could, in fact would, be a better place one day. As the school year drew to a close, I was almost convinced that once we unleashed April and her like-minded comrades on the world, that by September, we would surely return to a future in which universal peace and harmony were close at hand.

What about you? Do you remember what it was like to be idealistic? Do you recall how palpable and vigorous your convictions were? How doubtless your belief that if people would just sit down and talk with one another, reason with one another — love one another — that they would learn to transcend every artificially imposed barrier and find solutions to humankind's most daunting problems? Those of war and starvation, pollution and oppression, and all the other plagues of man.

Now ask yourself this — was that really you? Or was that just a naive and unseasoned version of your present grown-up self? Was there anything to that idealism, or was it just the immature folly and patently unrealistic dream stuff of youth?

How about this. Have you ever felt more free than when you were attuned to that part of you which said, "Somehow, someway, I know we can change this world." Deep down we all know that those rumblings, those dreams, that enthusiastically fresh idealism, stemmed from a very real part of who we are. Deep within our souls we are all idealists.

When pondering the creation of the first human being, the Talmud asks the following question: "Why was the first human created alone?" To which it replies, "So that each person should say — *the world was created for me.*" Far from justifying any and every abuse — *"hey, if it was created for me I can do whatever I want with it"* — this supremely Jewish idea says: It's your world and you're responsible for it! There is a voice, a subtle yet persistent voice, which tells us all that we are here for a reason. It tells us that we can, and must, make a difference.

Scrubbing The Floors Of Freedom

A funny thing happens on the way to Utopia. We grow up. We mature and learn that there is a real world out there; that you've got to be realistic, practical, and pragmatic about life. That little has changed over the millennia and that it's time you assumed some adult responsibilities; that the best you can hope for is to have a secure career, raise a nice family, perhaps make a contribution to your community, and then join your friends at the pool on Saturday.

This is what cleaning for Passover is all about. You see, as we abandon our dreams we abandon ourselves. In the process we consign our freedom to the trust of societal norms and thus we become enslaved. Slowly, without even noticing, we give up. We shelve our idealism and with it the hope of an empowered life of self-leadership. A life lived to its fullest.

This is not a suggestion to entirely reject everything the present "establishment" stands for — though it is a plea for integration. For finding a way to reinstate confidence in our human potential — our Jewish potential — indeed, in the framework of the real world. Because when we surrendered our souls to the comforts of convention, small cracks began to appear in our hearts' resolve. With time these cracks became gaping fissures of emptiness. An emptiness which begged to be filled.

And this filler has a name. We call it *chometz.*[*] Chometz is a great generic monster which grafts itself onto our being, insinuates itself into our consciousness, and becomes the focus of our thoughts, desires, and life's activities. When we give up on idealism for the sake of monetary gain, we acquire chometz. When we squelch our search for achievements of enduring value and opt

---

[*] *Chometz* is the Hebrew word for leaven. The purpose of Passover cleaning is to rid one's home of all traces of *chometz*. Symbolically, *chometz* represents the unproductive directions in which our lives often wander.

for the vicarious pleasure of watching others pursue victory, we acquire chometz. Whenever we settle for less and lose sight of what really matters, this too is chometz.

Chometz is bread and matzah is a form of bread, though matzah isn't chometz. In essence, bread comes from the same simple mixture of flour and water which matzah comes from. Only bread contains extra additives for taste and appearance, and is also afforded time to rise. Time to expand to the point where its potential to be matzah has become totally lost.

As Passover approaches we rid our homes of the dough that became bread in favor of the dough that became matzah. But beyond seeking out the crumbs in our homes we are told to take a searing look within ourselves. To see if we can't root out those insidious additives which have filled the cracks in our souls, and commandeered the passion of our lives. When we divest ourselves of this presence — if only for a week — then what we will rediscover is our basic selves. Our optimism, our idealism and our freedom. You guessed it — matzah!

III
FREEDOM, FREE WILL AND RESPONSIBILITY

A Longing For Freedom

Of our myriad drives and desires, yearnings and inclinations, few are as passionate and compelling as the drive for freedom. Freedom is a state of mind. Even more, it is a state of being so essential to human existence that without it the fabric of our lives is bereft of quality, color, and texture.

Children instinctively chase a freedom that is as frightening as it is exciting. Youth defies authority at every turn to pursue the helter skelter winds of freedom. They don't even know what they will do once they have it — but they know — they must have their freedom. Adults too, still yearning and longing, bolt the confines of career and family. All for freedom.

Thinkers from every discipline ponder and probe the meaning of freedom. Leaders call upon its power to inspire, and masses rise up to fight and die for it. And finally, America. That ennobled bearer of a torch held high to the huddled masses. At its idyllic best she serves as a humble beacon for all mankind. The land of the *free* and the home of the brave.

What Is Freedom?

Freedom is the capacity to express in one's life those values and ideals which stem from the essence of the human soul.

The Talmud says, *"Precious is the human being who was created in the image of G-d. And an even greater sign of this preciousness is that man was informed that he was created in G-d's image."* That all human beings are created in the image of G-d does not mean that there is a bit of Aphrodite and Adonis in all of us, but that we all have free will. All human beings possess the ability to make meaningful and substantive choices which have a direct impact on their lives, as well as on the lives of others. It is these choices which determine the ultimate moral and spiritual quality of every human being's existence.

Free Will And Responsibility

Everyone knows that people have the ability to make choices.

If you ever did something wrong — and later regretted it — then you believe you had a choice. If you ever felt that a criminal deserved to be punished — despite the socioeconomic factors he was subjected to — then you believe in free will. If you believe that Raoul Wallenberg[*] was a noble and righteous human being, then it's because you believe that he made a choice where so many others failed. And, if you ever yell at your kids for leaving their room a mess, then you most definately believe in free will. What you do not believe is that people are bound by the fatalistic chains

[*] A Swedish diplomat who acted courageously to save between 20,000 and 100,000 Hungarian Jews from the Germans in World War II.

of familial circumstance, socioeconomic condition, genes, or Divine predestination. Thus, you are not prisoner to an attitude of indifference, resignation, and melancholy. Instead you are animated by an abundantly optimistic outlook which sees self and others as shapers, creators and captains of great ships of potential.

You believe — as Judaism asserts — that people are people and not psychological robots. That the existence of free will automatically creates human responsibility. And, that the most precious gift a person can receive is the freedom to make their own choices, and to be responsible for their own actions.

Avoiding Freedom

There are many reasons why people shy away from choosing the freedom of being responsible. Here we will address two of the most common. (1) The reason we don't effectively use our free will to live responsibly is because we never bother to clarify our core values and goals in life. This results in our being totally oblivious to some of our most critical personal choices, even when they stare us right in the face. (2) When we do achieve a degree of self-awareness and clarity, still, we recoil at the painful prospect of exercising our free will, making tough choices, and assuming the full onus of responsibility.

Choice Management

Today it seems that business and the hyper-speed of technological advances are the metaphor for life. While there is something unsettling about seeing myself as a corporation, my mind as software, and my children as long-term investments, the fact is that the sages of the Talmud also viewed the workings of the business world as a useful paradigm for personal growth and character development.

The following model is designed to help you identify the

values central to your life and to then define a set of goals based on those values.* Additionally, it will assist you in charting a realistic course for achieving your goals and sensitize you to the critical choices which you must confront in order to live responsibly and achieve freedom.

This model is structured around a four-step process of introspection, projection, and planning. It is straightforward, easy to use, and *not* set in stone. It is based on the Jewish discipline of *cheshbon hanefesh*, personal choice management, and recognizes that ultimately everyone has to devise a customized approach which works best for them. It should be viewed as one way of doing things. The goal here is to provide a useful point of reference from which you can go on to develop your own personalized system.

STEP I   **Make a list of five values or ideals which you want to express in the way you live your life.**

A partial list of values and ideals:

Accepting	Energetic	Humorous	Modest
Responsible	Active	Empowering	Harmony
Make a difference	Self-aware	Appreciative	Flexible
Honest	Mature	Self-motivated	Assertive
Friendship	Helpful	Objective	Sensitive
Balanced	Fulfillment	Idealistic	Open-minded
Sincere	Communicative	Forgiving	Integrity
Organized	Truth-seeking	Compassionate	Gentle
Industrious	Patient	Understanding	Consistent
Giving	Independent	Peace of mind	Warm
Contributing	Grateful	Initiative	Peaceful
Daring	Growth-oriented	Joyful	Persevere

---

* It is not necessary to complete these exercises in order to continue with the rest of the book.

Decisive	Go-getter	Kind	Encouraging
Learner	Happy	Love	Positive influence
Efficient	Respect	Diligent	Resilient
Positive attitude	Humanitarian	Listener	Humble

STEP II   **List five spheres of life which you are most involved in, and/or in which you would like to qualitatively enhance your experience.**

A partial list of life spheres:

Business	Spouse	Relatives	Judaism
Children	Education	Friends	Career
Community	Synagogue	Self	Strangers
Health	Spirituality	Job	
G-d	Colleagues	Personal growth	

STEP III   **(A) Match a value/ideal to each of the five life spheres. This should be a value which you want to be ever-present in that sphere of your life. (B) Write a one-sentence statement which captures how your chosen value would be ideally expressed over the next twenty years. This is your goal for that sphere of life.**

STEP IV   **List two or three concrete objectives which, if met, you believe will result in the achievement of the goal stated in Step III.**

Examples:

1. Sphere of life: Marriage.
   Value/Ideal: Love.
   Goal: Our relationship will be characterized by a continual deepening of our love.

Objectives: (1) Spend one hour of private time together twice a week.
(2) Keep a list of "things I love" about my husband/wife next to my bed and add to it once a week.
(3) Say "thank you" once a day for a routine activity.

II. Sphere of life: Business.
     Value/Ideal: Honesty.
     Goal: My reputation should be, "His word is as good as gold."
     Objectives: (1) Incorporate the following statement into my vocabulary. "If I make a commitment, I stand by it, so let me think about what we just said and I'll get back to you in an hour."
(2) After describing a product or service to a customer or client, I will ask myself, "If I were my client, would I feel satisfied with this purchase?"

III. Sphere of life: Judaism.
     Value/Ideal: Growth-oriented.
     Goal: To posses the type of Jewish knowledge that will enable me to give my children a good feeling about being Jewish.
     Objectives: (1) Read four Jewish books a year.
(2) To compile a list of my questions about Judaism and ask different rabbis for answers.

When The Going Gets Tough

When one begins to see life as an ongoing process of making choices and accepting responsibility, then there is no escaping the reality that life is always tough. That's just the way it is. Embracing this fact is the first step in overcoming the hurdle of avoiding choices because of the pain involved.

The second step is to realize that it's a pleasure to be tough. We all know that those accomplishments which have most enriched our lives were possible only because of the effort involved, the discomfort endured and the difficult decisions which had to be made. This is a quid pro quo known to Judaism as *L'fum tzara agra*, which means, *according to the effort is the reward*. The reason mountain climbers aren't lowered to the summit by a helicopter is because the reward — the satisfaction, pleasure, growth, sense of meaning, and thrill — are all a direct result of a challenging climb. What's more, the climb itself *is* the pleasure. Being forced to abandon an imminent assault on the summit by a sudden snowstorm will never engender regret in the heart of one who tries to scale Everest. Because the reward *is* the effort.

Our tradition has it that only 20 percent of the Jewish people left Egypt. The other 80 percent died and were buried during the plague of darkness. Why did they die? Because they weren't prepared to make the choice of freedom. When push came to shove they preferred the familiar routine of slavery to the unknown challenges of the desert.

Judaism says: life is about choosing; choosing is difficult and life is a pleasure. This Passover, make a commitment to the pleasure of tough choices, and whatever you do — don't get left behind.

IV
GOD AND FREEDOM: THE ODD COUPLE

Let's face it, anyone who knows anything about the Jewish holiday cycle knows that just seven weeks after being freed from bondage in Egypt the Jewish nation stood at the foot of Mount Sinai.

When Moses petitioned Pharaoh in Egypt, he spoke in the name of G-d and said, *"G-d has sent me to tell you, 'Let my people go, so that they may serve me in the desert'*. And sure enough, barely two months after leaving Egypt, there they were in the desert receiving not just ten, but six hundred and thirteen *mitzvot* (commandments). Two hundred and forty-eight positive, three hundred and sixty-five negative, and all of them with hundreds of details about how, when, and where to carry out each individual command. So much for freedom!

*   *   *

A young prodigy enters the hallowed halls of Julliard. She is subjected to a grueling regimen of instruction and practice followed by more instruction and more practice. Guided by the erudite vision and steady hand of a maestro, the student is carefully led through a progression conceived by masters. It is all part of the careful development of musical talent and technique. The discipline is exacting, the demands are great, and the rules are to be strictly adhered to. And the goal of all this is freedom. The nurtured freedom of spontaneous expressions of genius.

The untrained eye sees only the effortlessness of silken spontaneity. It all looks so easy. Like Michael Jordan. So smooth that kids everywhere think that all they need is the right pair of sneakers and they too will be able to perform airborne ballet steps with a basketball.

It's true, genius is a gift, but greatness is an achievement. All the G-d-given talents in the world will never budge from the realm of potential if they aren't harnessed, molded, developed, and guided. This is exactly why masters, mentors, and basketball coaches, though appearing to tie their charges in one knot after another, are indispensable instruments of freedom. They unlock potential, liberate talents, and create the dynamics necessary for the expression of seemingly effortless spontaneity and creativity.

Spirituality And Spontaneity

In the eyes of the Torah, every Jew is a spiritual prodigy. At the Shabbat meal on Friday night Jewish parents bless their sons — *"that they may be like Ephraim and Menashe"* — and their daughters — *"that they may be like Sarah, Rebecca, Rachel, and Leah."* Greatness of character, spirit, and moral fiber, are the stuff every Jewish child is made of. In blessing our daughters to be like Sarah, we are not praying that they should become another Sarah— for there can never be another Sarah. Instead we pray that just as Sarah's life was a remarkable expression of one woman's potential, such should be the destination of all our children. That they might invest their best efforts in an ennobled encounter with the special circumstances of their existence and therein nourish the imaginable while making possible the unimaginable.

As Jews set out to confront life, it is with G-d as our coach and the *mitzvot* as a discipline of spiritual directives. This system of spiritual directives works to simultaneously harness and liberate the spontaneity of the human spirit in the dance of life. As detailed and far reaching as the *mitzvot* may be, when set against the situational matrix of life, they are recast as indispensable sign posts which hone our intuition as they indicate the direction in which we are to go — and grow.

The Torah says, *"Be careful to observe the mitzvot of Hashem your G-d, and His ordinances, and His statutes, as He has commanded you. And you should do what is straight and good in the eyes of G-d."*[*] There is a perplexing side to this exhortation to carefully fulfill the commandments in the Torah. How could it be that after being told to *"be careful to observe the mitzvot"* that there is still room to say *"do what is straight and good?"* Are the qualities of *straightness* and *goodness* not requisite to a life of *mitzvah*-observance? Is a *mitzvah* still identifiable as a *mitzvah* if it is devious and corrupt? What the Torah is alluding to here is the fact that even after one is committed to observing all 613 *mitzvot*,

---

[*] Deut. 6:17 – 18. See the commentary of Nachmonides (Ramban).

there is much in life which is left unaddressed. In all those instances, be they interpersonal, professional, religious, or otherwise, the Torah is saying that each individual must be the ultimate arbitor of what is *straight* and *good*. The responsibility of living a life shaped by straightness and goodness is laid clearly at our doorstep. At the same time, we are not left directionless.

George Bernard Shaw said, *"Only on paper has humanity yet achieved glory, beauty, truth, knowledge, virtue and abiding love."* The *mitzvot* are études of character. Like a Chopin piano piece that works to blend refined technical skills with musical harmony, the *mitzvot* act as living mediums through which our latent capacities for growth are transferred from paper potential to the sturdy material of everyday life.

To think that it is easy to be a Jew because Jewish observance and practice dictate the course of one's every action is to be blind to the scope of each individual's potentialities; to the value, quality, and sanctity inherent in every nuance of living, and to the presence of meaning in all encounters with things external to the self. From the *straightness* and *goodness* which animate the 613 overt *mitzvot* we can infer countless other mitzvaesque approaches to the ever unfolding variables which an interactive life calls upon us to address.

The Paradox Of Commanded Freedom

The acceptance of the Torah by the Jewish people at Mount Sinai was not a repudiation of the freedom achieved at the exodus. These were not slaves, and the sons of slaves, who sought to exchange one hopeless yoke for another. These were — or better — this *is* a people who well understand that unharnessed potential is potential squandered. That an undirected life is a carelessly gambled life, and that the dimunition of thoughtful rules and disciplines are open invitations, not to human freedom, but to savage anarchy.

Thus, the acceptance of the *mitzvot*. A system of spiritual mechanisms designed to educate and sensitize us to the qualities of straightness and goodness which are attainable in life. Still, even more than being carefully crafted means to a beautiful end, each *mitzvah* is also a deeply meaningful end in itself.

When a third-year resident assists in a major surgical procedure, that's not called practice — that's reality, and that's for keeps. Similarly, each *mitzvah* stands independently as an experiential moment of growth, insight, and spiritual connectedness.[*] And, at the same time, it lays the groundwork for the future realization of enormous potential. As Johannes Brahms said, *"Without craftsmanship, inspiration is a mere reed shaken in the wind."*

---

[*] For an exploration of the relevancies of specific *mitzvot*, see *The Nineteen Letters* by Samson Raphael Hirsch, and its companion volume, *Horeb*.

5

HOW TO SURVIVE THE SEDER

The three keys to surviving the Seder are (1) educational preparedness, (2) creativity, and (3) a commitment to making it a meaningful experience for everyone involved.

The following ideas will speak to three people: (1) the person or people who are hosting the Seder, (2) parents of young children, and (3) someone who will be a guest at a Seder. These ideas are by no means exhaustive. Clearly, every family and every Seder is unique. This means that the ultimate success and quality of any Seder will be directly proportional to the effort put into appropriately blending the three keys mentioned above. Like all other worthwhile endeavors, an enriching and uplifting Seder does not come easily. Nor does it come all at once. But I promise you — 100 percent, money-back, no questions asked, guarantee you — that if you accept the challenge of developing your Seder in the ways which this book suggests, that as the years go by, you will find that your dining room is no longer large enough to hold all the people who will want to be a part of your Seder. And that's a promise.

I.   **The host/leader of the Seder.**

1.   You must develop a well-thought-out game plan for running the Seder. This begins with your accepting the pleasurable burden of becoming the resident Passover expert. At the very least, you should try to read the entire *Survival Kit* well in advance of the Seder. Ideally, you will read one other Haggadah with commentary and explanations. Secondly, you must think about who your guests will be and ask what it will take to make the Seder enjoyable and meaningful for them.

2.   Establish a creative partnership. A week or two before Passover, call your guests and ask them to study up on a particular paragraph in the Haggadah. Ask them to ask themselves the following question: What idea(s) is contained in this paragraph which people would find interesting, thought-provoking and insightful?

3.   Don't give everyone at your Seder the same Haggadah, and don't give out Haggadahs that have only the text and no commentary. (Don't look at this idea as an expense, look at it as an investment.)

4.   There is no such thing as a dumb question. Encourage an atmosphere in which people feel comfortable to ask questions about what's being said in the Haggadah. Once a question is asked, invite everyone to think about a possible answer, and/or to look in their Haggadah to find one.

5. Be flexible and alter your game plan where necessary.

6. Questions of identity. Since Passover marks the birth of the Jewish nation, it is a good time to encourage people to reflect on the meaning, value, and implications of their Jewishness. Here are some sample questions you can present at the Seder.

    i.   On a scale of 1–10, how important is being Jewish to you? Please explain.
    ii. If your son, daughter, brother, sister, cousin, or best friend told you that they planned to raise their children without any Jewish education or identity, how would you react?
    iii. If you thought the existence of Israel was in danger, would you risk your life to help save it?
    iv. What do you like about being Jewish? What don't you like?
    v.   Is it important to you to have — or for your children to have — mostly Jewish friends?

Note: As important as it is that people feel comfortable to ask their questions, the friendly, nonjudgmental atmosphere you want to create also requires that people feel comfortable enough to decline a response when asked a question.

II. Parents with children at the Seder.

1. The plagues.
    Start a collection of visual aids for the Passover Seder. You can add to this collection year round. Some examples. (1) Ping-pong balls work great for the plague of hail. The more the merrier. (2) Halloween is a good time to find inexpensive "wild beast" masks for

the fourth plague. (3) Frogs and locusts can be found at the nature store in your local shopping mall. Be creative!

2. Passover storybooks.
    For a couple of weeks before Passover, read your kids Passover stories at night. It is also a good idea to find a book about Passover which can be read at the dinner table every night as Passover approaches.

3. Based on what you have read with your children, you can now ask questions at the Seder which they will be able to answer. This excites them, makes them feel good about themselves, and is a wonderful source of *nachas* for the grandparents.
    You can have little prizes to give out for correct answers. After a while you'll see that the adults will want prizes too. Go ahead, it's part of the fun.
    Caution: Be sensitive to the children of guests. Find ways to include them too.

4. A short skit. Write a short skit about the exodus from Egypt. Characters can include Moses, Pharaoh, G-d, a firstborn Egyptian, a Jewish slave, an Egyptian taskmaster, a wild beast, etc. Short written scripts can be given to each child (adults too if they want). Give the kids your full attention — they are the stars of the show.

5. Find the patterns.
    i.   The number four is significant on Passover (see page 27) and there are numerous instances of things appearing in groupings and patterns of four.

The most well known are the *four* questions and the *four* sons — though there are many others. Everytime someone notices a pattern of four, give them a toothpick. The one with the most toothpicks at the end gets a prize. Try to find a way to make everyone a winner — we certainly don't want anyone to feel like a loser on Passover.

ii. One of the primary themes woven into the text of the Haggadah is gratitude (see page 65). The same type of game as above can be played with identifying sentences or paragraphs which contain the message of gratitude.

6. Sticker madness. Jewish bookstores carry a variety of colorful Passover stickers. These can be a lot of fun when incorporated into the Seder as prizes for asking or answering a question, noticing a pattern, reading a paragraph in the Haggadah, etc. They can also be used to keep the children excited about fulfilling the *mitzvot* at the Seder. When they eat matzah they get a matzah sticker, for maror they get a bitter herb sticker, and so on.

III. **When you are a guest.**

1. You've read the *Passover Survival Kit* six times, purchased and plowed through three other Haggadahs, and are eager to have the most profound Seder experience of your life. One problem — you know that at the Seder you annually attend they will still be locked into the *"can we hurry up and get to dinner already"* syndrome. So what do you do?

i. Reread the second half of the first chapter of this book, "Survival Kit User's Guide."

ii. Read the *Survival Kit* before going to the Seder
and highlight those sections which you want to be
sure and think about during the Seder.

iii. Think about who will be at the Seder and make
notes of any ideas in the *Survival Kit* which you
think the group, or a particular individual, will
relate to. At the appropriate time you can say, "Hey
Uncle Harry, it says something here I think you
would really appreciate."

iv. Bring an extra copy of the *Survival Kit* to the Seder.
Inevitably someone will be intrigued by your
radical departure from the old Maxwell House
Haggadahs. They will want to look at yours, and if
you don't have an extra one on hand, that may be
the last you will see of it.

2. Get the kids involved. You can bring stickers or
Passover candies and introduce the game of "patterns
of four" or "gratitude." Before the Seder begins tell
your host that you have some great ideas for keeping
the kids involved. Generally they will be very receptive
and before you know it, everyone will be involved.

6

THE PASSOVER PUZZLE: FIFTEEN SEQUENTIAL EXPERIENCES

An Overview of the Seder

From beginning to end, the Seder is comprised of fifteen specific experiences. These fifteen segments of the Seder follow a precise order and each comes with its own set of instructions.

It is a good idea for the leader of the Seder to take a few minutes and give a brief overview of these fifteen segments. This will provide people with a general framework for the Seder and give them a sense that the evening is following a purposeful pattern and not just wandering from ritual to ritual. It is also interesting to point out that the Hebrew word *seder* actually means *order*, and relates to the fact that the Seder follows a precise order, or pattern, which is embodied in these fifteen experiences. In fact, over the centuries many great scholars have revealed a wealth of ideas which illuminate a deeper meaning to these fifteen sequential experiences and how they are interrelated. Some of these ideas will be touched upon in the coming pages.

Before proceeding to *kiddush*, the blessing over the first cup of wine, it is customary for everyone at the Seder to sing or read the list of the fifteen observances.

1. **Kadesh**   A special blessing is recited over a glass of wine or grape juice. This blessing speaks of the treasured role which all holidays play in Jewish life and makes particular reference to the unique opportunity embodied in Passover.

2. **Urechatz**   Prior to eating the *karpas* (vegetable), everyone at the Seder washes their hands in the prescribed manner. Unlike the washing which will precede the eating of the matzah, no blessing is made at this point.

3. **Karpas**   A small piece of vegetable is dipped in salt water and then eaten.

4. **Yachatz**   The person leading the Seder takes the middle matzah and breaks it in half. The larger half becomes the afikomen and the smaller half is returned to its place.

5. **Maggid**   This is the reading and discussion of the Haggadah text. At least half of the Seder is devoted to the telling of the exodus from Egypt. The emphasis here is on educating Jewish children as to the meaning of their history and identity as well as probing the text for ideas that relate to the theme of freedom.

6. **Rachtzah**   After completing the Haggadah, everyone washes their hands before eating the matzah and beginning the meal. A blessing is recited by each individual after washing his or her hands.

7. **Motzi**   This is the blessing said anytime one eats bread or matzah.

8. *Matzah*   A piece of matzah is eaten in accordance with the commandment to eat matzah on the night of Passover. A blessing is recited before eating.

9. *Maror*   A blessing is said, and the bitter herbs are eaten.

10. *Korech*   Having just eaten matzah and bitter herbs separately, we now eat them together as a sandwich.

11. *Shulchan Orech*   Finally! The festive Passover meal is enjoyed by all.

12. *Tzafon*   The afikomen, which had been hidden earlier, is now brought back and everyone eats a piece of matzah as their own personal afikomen.

13. *Barech*   This blessing is said at the conclusion of every meal. Tonight it contains special references to Passover.

14. *Hallel*   Reciting the songs of praise authored by King David.

15. *Nirtzah*   We pray that we have successfully fulfilled all the observances of the Seder. We seal our hopes for a brighter future with the words, *"Next year in Jerusalem."*

*   *   *

The remaining portion of this chapter contains some of the ideas which underlie the fifteen Seder experiences. The leader of the Seder should be acquainted with their meaning before the evening begins. This will allow him to provide a brief explanation of each step as it arises. Alternatively, either the leader or various guests can read the appropriate explanations at the time of the observance.

*   *   *

THE PASSOVER PUZZLE

The holiday of Passover is known as *Zman Cheruteynu* — the time of our freedom. And it is the Passover Seder, that most durable and popular of all Jewish practices, which is the pivotal component of this week-long "time of our freedom." The Seder itself is composed of fifteen carefully fashioned pieces. This Seder, like the emergent picture formed by the pieces of some fantastic jigsaw puzzle, is designed to create a vivid experiential image of what freedom is all about. But these are no ordinary puzzle pieces as this is no ordinary puzzle. This is a puzzle in which the pieces are affected by the way they are held. It is through the careful and precise handling of each piece that its inherent form begins to emerge. Further, it is our thoughts and understanding of the intrinsic nature of these rebus-like pieces which serve to reveal their true color, imagery, and light. Once assembled, they create a brilliant mosaic of freedom.

And what a spectacular creation this freedom can be. That sense of profound inner confidence and strength of character born of a conviction to pursue a meaningful, spiritual, and moral existence. The freedom of a Jewish soul. A soul guided by wisdom and inspired by everything we have ever stood for. This vibrant totality becomes visible through the piece by piece assembly of the Seder experience, and in turn works its way into the very fabric of our being.

The ideas which follow are merely a glimpse into the world of insight contained in each one of the fifteen pieces of the Passover puzzle. Thousands of volumes have been written, each one exploring another facet of Passover, the Haggadah, and the pieces of the Seder. It is my hope that the ideas related here will serve as a relevant starting point as you approach your experience at the Seder, your assembly of these marvelous pieces of wisdom and your Passover odyssey in freedom.

1. *Kadesh*. The recitation of the *kiddush* blessing over a glass of wine or grape juice.

The words *kadesh* and *kiddush* are derived from the word *kadosh*. Though commonly translated as "holy" or "sanctified," *kadosh* actually means *separate* or *distinct*.

The first piece in our puzzle — *Kadesh* — summons us to step into the distinctive world of Passover. A world filled with feelings, *mitzvot,* (commandments), customs, and ideas, all of which point the way to freedom. This very act of separation begins to move us towards a deeper awareness of ourselves and what it will take to achieve the prized freedom of Passover.

Sometimes, "just getting away from things" is precisely what is needed to gain a fresh perspective on the situation of our lives. By separating ourselves from routine, we are able to reflect on where we are, how we got there, what's driving us, and what our goals are. Then, with a bit more clarity, we can address the question, "Where do we go from here?"

On the Seder night we "get away" to a place filled with Jewish ideas about freedom and about life. From there we look back and imagine a life empowered by our noblest inclinations and vivified by a commitment to making the world the kind of place Judaism believes it can be.

2. *Urechatz*. Washing the hands before eating the karpas.

> Ask someone which comes first, the house or the blueprints. The answer you are most likely to receive is "the blueprints, of course." The truth, however, is quite the opposite. In a song which is sung at the Friday evening Shabbat service we find the words, *soaf ma-aseh bemachshava techillah,* which means, *every goal must precede itself in thought*. First comes a completed house in conceptual form — the goal — and only then are blueprints drawnup and a house finally built.

Today it is the practice to wash one's hands only before eating bread or matzah, but when the Temple stood in Jerusalem, Jews also washed before eating other types of foods. The washing before the *karpas* is reminiscent of life at that time. After having entered the dimension of Passover by way of the *kiddush, urechatz* now tells us to stop and focus on another time and on other goals. Because freedom is not the license to gratify impulses on demand, but the state of mastering the range of one's drives and powers. Only then is the full force of one's being brought to bear on the realization of his or her ultimate goals.

This is Jerusalem. More than just the seat of Jewish national sovereignty, the restored Jerusalem we have always dreamt of is one from which all mankind are to draw inspiration and wisdom. It is the embodiment of our goals and our mission. Born in the darkness of Egypt, we have been called to be *"a light unto the nations."* A spiritual conduit, with Jerusalem as the nexus, through which enlightenment will come to the world.

Jerusalem, with the Temple at its heart, is where we develop our most intimate relationship with a sublime Creator. From there we are stirred to translate the energy of that relationship into a passionate pursuit of our goals as a people. The dream of Jerusalem — the dream of humankind achieving a state where it is both human and kind — is the dream of every Jewish soul.

Right from the start *urechatz* tells us to lift our eyes and gaze at a vision of our ultimate goals. Because — *every goal must precede itself in thought*.

Another piece in the puzzle, and another move towards freedom.

3. *Karpas*. We dip a piece of vegetable in salt water and eat it.

I. Close your eyes and picture someone who you consider to be a beautiful human being. Someone who imbodies the finest qualities a person can possess.

II. Having done so, now ask yourself if it isn't that person's capacity to be a giver which allows you to identify him or her as beautiful. Their penchant for being outwardly focused and other-centered. To be benevolent and compassionate. To be sincerely concerned with the well-being of others.

We are transfixed by the artist's talent, carried away by the virtuoso's melody and envious of the Fortune 500 C.E.O. Yet the quality of beauty is not one we necessarily attach to any of these men or women of achievement. But we do intuitively associate giving with beauty, and thus, almost instinctively, we try to raise children who are "givers" and not "takers." After all, is there anyone who could proudly state, "my son the taker"? A doctor, a professor, an athlete, or even an author — but none at the expense of being a self-centered taker.

Hebrew: The Fantasia of Language

In the Hebrew language every letter is not only a letter, but also a number, a word, and a concept. As an example, the letter *aleph*, the first letter of the alphabet, has the numerical value of one. *Aleph* is also a word which means to champion, or to lead. The second letter of the alphabet, *beit*, has the numerical value of two and also means house, or *bayit* , in Hebrew. Hebrew letters, then, are far more than mere letters, but are actually linguistic repositories for numerous concepts and ideas. Words, too, become not only an amalgam of random sounds but precise constructs of the conceptual components of the object with which the word is associated.

When we analyze the word *karpas* and break it down to its four component parts — its four letters — what we discover is an encoded message which teaches a basic lesson about how to develop our capacity for giving.

The Hebrew word *karpas* is constructed of four letters; *kaf, reish, peh,* and *samech.* These four letters are also four words, and when taken together they steer our mind's eye towards an essential aspect of giving.

K (a)*	⟹	*Kaf* =	Palm of hand.
R	⟹	*Reish* =	One who is impoverished.
P (a)	⟹	*Peh* =	Mouth.
S	⟹	*Samech* =	To support.

The word *kaf*, the first letter in *karpas*, means the palm of the hand. This part of our anatomy is exposed when the hand is open — in a giving mode. The word *reish* means a poor person. When taken together these first two letter/words speak of a benevolent hand opened for the needy. Thus we have the classic image of giving; one who has more, lending assistance to one who has less. But what if you are a person of limited means? What if you simply have precious little to give? The second half of the word *karpas* reminds us that there are many roads to becoming a giver. The letter *peh* means mouth, while the final letter *samech* means to support. True, you may not be capable of giving in the material sense, but you can always give with your words. Words of kindness and concern. Words of empathy and understanding. Words that can lift an impoverished soul and provide a means of support where nothing else will do.

*   *   *

We dip the karpas in saltwater. The saltwater is meant to recall the bitter tears shed in Egypt. But there is more. The Jewish people, though awash in the tears of bondage, were able to preserve their ability to give. Rather then succumb to the morass of self-pity, they were able to maintain their dignity by maintaining their beauty. The beauty born of giving.

> **?** 1. Besides teaching your kids to share with siblings and friends, what will you do to instill in them the quality of giving?
>
> 2. Which posture will contribute more to the

---

* Hebrew is a consonantal alphabet. Vowel sounds are represented as diacritics and not as individual letters.

accomplishment of your most important life goals —
that of the giver or that of the taker?

3. Did you — or will you — enter marriage looking
more to bestow or to receive?

4. *Yachatz*. Break the middle piece of matzah. The smaller piece
is returned to its place while the larger one is wrapped and put
aside to serve later as the afikomen.

*If a friend needed to borrow one of our cars for a
couple of days, I'm sure my wife and I would try to
be accommodating. On the other hand, if they
needed it for a month or two, we would have to
apologize and explain that we really can't manage
with just one car.*

*Recently something happened which forced us to
rethink this position. One of our cars broke down. And
it took a month to get the right parts! So how did we
deal with this suburban catastrophe? Did we rent, did
we borrow, did we steal? No. We simply managed.
With an adjustment here, some juggling over there,
and an added bit of patience all around, we were able
to adjust our schedules, give one another rides, make
alternative arrangements, and barely miss a beat in
our busy schedules. We also had the pleasure of some
extra time together.*

*Funny, isn't it? There are so many things which we
simply "can't live without," until, of course we have
to. But mind you, our new bread maker is a different
story all together. We really can't live without that!*

So you want to be a giver, only you think you have nothing to
give. Not in the material sense and not even in the emotional or
spiritual sense. Well, think again. Quite often our inability to give
and to share is the product of a skewed picture of reality. Many of

our limitations are only perceived limitations. Fictitious barriers which many before us have overcome and others just like us will continue to surmount.

This is *yachatz*. The middle matzah is broken in two, the larger piece is hidden away, and the smaller piece returns to its place where it continues to fulfill its function despite the loss. No, this is not a suggestion that you go out and intentionally smash your second (or third) car, trade in your microwave for a Bunsen burner, or cut your sleeping hours in half, but it is a suggestion to pause.

If your brother or sister needed some of your time, money, or a piece of your heart, would you not find a way to give it to them? Humankind is a family and Jews are all brothers and sisters. Just as there are plenty of needs, there are also plenty of resources. If only we realized how much we had to give, and how much we truly want to give.

> ? Imagine this: One day you get a phone call. Your relatives from Russia have just arrived with their three children. No money, no possessions, they don't speak the language, the local federation has exhausted its funds, and they are counting on you. What would you do?

5. *Maggid*. Read and discuss the text of the Haggadah.

Would it really be such a big deal if parents never taught their children to say "thank you"? Obviously it would be, because if you don't say thank you, you're an ingrate. And just like no one wants to be an ingrate, no one wants to marry one, be friends with one, or raise one. Thus, the "magic words" — thank you.

All ingrates end up in prison. Their ego-obsessed lack of gratitude erects impenetrable walls which lock the world out and shut the ingrate in.

The Talmud teaches that the thematic flow of the Haggadah narrative is meant to sensitize us to one of life's most basic traits of self-liberation. Gratitude. The textual flow of the Haggadah follows a pattern known as *"opening with the ignominious and concluding with the praiseworthy."* It is for this reason that the Haggadah begins by highlighting the less-than-flattering origins of the Jewish people — *"we were slaves to Pharaoh in Egypt... Our forefathers were idol worshippers...* — and concludes with our triumphant liberation and the formation of a relationship with G-d. This recurrent theme of contrasting lowly origins with ennobled achievements is meant to sensitize us to that trait which stands as the ingrate's staunchest rival — gratitude.

Those successful men and women who forget their humble origins and eschew the commoners who helped them achieve their success are doomed to occupy a cell, plush though it may be, inhabited only by themselves and a gaggle of smiling opportunists *cum* friends. As ingratitude builds walls, *thank you*, two truly magical words, are able to build bridges. From man to man and from man to G-d.

Toda: *Another Look at Thank You*

The Hebrew word for "thank you" is *toda*, which means *to admit*. When we say thank you we are making an admission. We admit that we needed someone else. You passed me the salt, helped me in business, changed my tire, or raised me as a child. To say thank you means to admit that "I couldn't have done it without you." Beneath it all, when we express our gratitude, be it to man or G-d, we are recognizing our dependence on another and acknowledging the kind assistance we have received. And though dependence is never easy to admit — when graciously acknowledged — it facilitates harmony, bonding, and freedom.

6. *Rachtzah*. Washing the hands prior to eating the matzah.

With one-third of our pieces in place, and another two-thirds waiting to be assembled, *rachtzah* prompts us to focus on an essential perspective necessary to attaining the freedom of Passover. This is the awareness of our ability to make changes in life. To cleanse ourselves of corrosive habits which stymie our efforts for fulfilled living. If life is about growth and growth means change, then, to pick up where one sixties-era lyricist left off, *Freedom's just another word... for change*! Or, as William James put it, *"The greatest discovery of my generation is that a human being can alter his life by altering his attitude."*

Rachtzah is exactly what it appears to be. It is a washing away of those rusty attitudinal routines which threaten to lock our lives into a holding pattern for mediocrity. There may be nothing more liberating than recognizing the possibility of liberation. The realization that one is capable of change and growth qualitatively alters the rules of the game. Where once the deck seemed to be stacked against us, the odds are now clearly in our favor.

7. *Motzi*. The blessing recited before eating the first piece of matzah.

The blessing we say for matzah is the same blessing we say before eating bread. "Blessed are you, Hashem, our G-d, King of the universe — *hamotzi lechem min ha-aretz* — who brings forth bread from the ground."

This blessing doesn't seem to be giving credit where credit is due. Granted, G-d may bring forth wheat from the ground, but when was the last time you saw a farmer harvesting loaves of bread? Bread comes from the ovens of bakers and *bubbies*, not "from the ground"! And, if you want to be a stickler about this, G-d doesn't even deserve all the credit for the wheat. Isn't the farmer the one who prepares the soil for planting, properly sows the seeds, and then harvests at just the right time? If anything, the production of bread and matzah is a partnership, with G-d acting as the junior partner.

There is an idea in *halacha* — Jewish law — which seems to reinforce the problem with the way the blessing of *hamotzi* is worded. The halacha states that upon saying *hamotzi* one should be careful to hold the loaf with all ten fingers. This is to remind us that the production of bread is a ten step process. From the preparation of the soil, to the planting, harvesting, grinding, and right through the kneading and baking of the dough, is a full ten steps. Aren't all of these steps in the hands of man, as the *halacha* implies, and not in the hands of G-d, as the blessing implies?

The Partnership of Man and G-d

When I floss my teeth and thereby forestall the creeping advances of tooth and gum decay, do I deserve a pat on the back and a round of applause? Do I hold my head high and flash a proud contented smile? Or, do I say,"thank G-d I've got the brains and ability to prevent my teeth from becoming premature mush."

Judaism says take pleasure — not pride — in the constructive choices you make in life. The Jewish view of the man – G-d partnership boils down to this. You make the sensible choice to floss your teeth: the rest is a gift. The cognitive aptitude necessary to grasp the hygienist's instructions on how to floss. The ability to consistently judge whether or not you've pulled out the right amount of floss. The dexterity required to gently maneuver the floss between tooth and gum. Each of these disparate abilities along with countless others are gifts from G-d.

A fresh loaf of bread, like a well-flossed tooth, is a marvelous accomplishment. We take pleasure in our accomplishments, and are thankful that we chose to use our many gifts in a constructive and meaningful manner.

8. *Matzah*. Eating the first piece of matzah.

9. *Maror*. Eating the bitter herbs.

10. *Korech*. Eating the sandwich of matzah and maror.

11. *Shulchan Orech*. Eating the festive meal.

12. *Tzafon* . Eating the afikomen, the hidden piece of matzah.

These five pieces of the Passover puzzle are each centered on eating and together form one suprapiece. When taken together, these pieces provide a sweeping view of the basic spiritual make-up of every human being. In doing so they simultaneously reveal a path for successfully engaging the ever-present physicality of our existence.

The Continuum of Human Spirituality

At one end of the spectrum of created beings there are purely spiritual entities. These are the angels. The other end is populated by purely physical beings. For instance, cows. The question is: where on this continuum do we fit in? "Well," you might think to yourself, "some people I know come close to that end, while others seem to belong to the end where grazing is the dominant activity of the day."

The Jewish concept is that human beings, unique creatures that we are, are a blend of both ends of the spectrum. That is, each and every one of us is part angel and part Holstein. Part spiritual and part physical.*

Take a look for yourself. Isn't there something within you — an angelic core — which is inclined towards the spiritual? Towards that which transcends the mundanity of the corporeal? A portion of your being which yearns to dispense with its

---

* This illustration is a simplification of an esoteric area of Jewish thought. It is beyond the scope of this work to deal with these ideas in an exhaustive manner.

preoccupation with food, sleep, and comfort. To free itself to pursue the eternal and not the transitory, to experience that which is intensely meaningful and not fleeting or petty.

Now look again. Is there not a part of you that longs to spend endless sun-massaged days on a quiet beach? Chilled beverages at your side, CDs playing your favorite music, the Sunday paper... and drift away... from all your cares, worries and responsibilities.

This is us. A not always so harmonious blend of spiritual and physical. One moment selflessly seeking to better the lot of all mankind, the next in a huff over the delivery of a pizza *without* the extra cheese. One day inspired to find private time to meditate or nurture our spousal intimacy, only to wake up at week's end buried by a heap of files labeled wealth, success, and acclaim. This is all of us. It is the conundrum of our existence and the dynamic to which the matzah and maror allude.

Matzah... is the soul. When pared of his or her external trappings and physical interests you will find that something yet remains of the human being. The longing of the soul. The basic nucleus of self. Likewise a loaf of bread. When denied all its additives; of sugar and salt, of poppy seeds or raisins, and even of time to rise, an essence still remains. Stripped-down bread is matzah and a stripped-down human being is a soul.

For an entire week we eat only matzah and consider only our deepest aspirations and loftiest dreams. Like an unwieldy corporate monster which has become diversified beyond recognition, we now attempt to get back to the basics. To focus not only on priorities but on the basic values and goals which define our priorities. Ultimately, to reconnect with that inner force which once promised to animate our every move.

Maror... is our physicality run amok. To demean the body and shun the world of physical pleasures is never the way of Judaism. Rather, Judaism asserts what all of us know. If you eat too much ice cream, you get sick; if you eat ice cream too fast, you won't taste it, and, if you eat too much ice cream, eventually you will lose your taste for ice cream.

The alternative, the Jewish path to both ice cream and spirituality, is to master our desires for the delicious. The bitter herbs are not a call to ascetic denial, but rather a reminder of one of life's earliest learned truths. That for a cow a life guided by moment-to-moment physical needs and urges is fine, perhaps even sweet, but for us — angels that we are — it can get a little bitter. Remember this lesson and you are halfway home to becoming an authentic connoisseur — of life.

Korech... is the most precise picture of who we are. We are neither the unencumbered soul of the Brahman nor the untamed body of a gluttonous boor. Rather, as two hydrogen atoms adhere to one of oxygen and form a new entity called water, so a soul when fused with a body becomes the crowning element of creation. A striving, struggling, growing, free-willed, creative human being. He who masters the tensions of this duality. He who can achieve a spiritually driven balance, who is able to live like a soul while dressing like a body is ready to move on....

... **to Shulchan Orech**. To a grand view of life which sees the world as an exquisitely set table of delicious opportunities for growth. A banquet without end. Know your essence, beware the bitter herbs, harmonize the totality of your being in the service of your greatest goals, then — and only then — will the delicacies of living truly be open to you.

Tzafon... means *concealment,* and depicts ultimate potential. We bring the afikomen out of its place of hiding and with it we bring a message of the hidden potential in every aspect of creation.

The afikomen represents the Passover lamb (see page) which was eaten by every Jew when the Temple stood in Jerusalem. The *halacha* (Jewish law) regarding the Passover lamb states (1) that it must be eaten only *after* the Passover meal has been concluded, and (2) that nothing may be eaten after the lamb. In effect, it is lamb chops and not macaroons which are the Passover dessert of tradition. Today the same rules apply to the afikomen. We eat it only after concluding our entire meal, and it is to be the last food we taste at the Seder. The afikomen is not consumed because we are hungry, but only because it is a *mitzvah*, a spiritual directive.

Generally when we eat, it is to satisfy our appetite — but not tonight. Tonight the afikomen points to eating not as an ends but as an enabler; to physical pleasures as an aid and not as an aim. Ultimately the intended state of the physical world is that of a vast toolshed overflowing with devices designed to access a higher reality. When properly understood, the hidden potential of our physicality is to connect us to a spiritual dimension stored in every corner of creation.

This is the secret of eating the hidden piece of matzah. Every aspect of life, every person and every fruit, every moment and every blade of grass, possesses ultimate potential. Like the latent forces of energy stored up in every atom, there is the potential of spirituality waiting inside every morsel of life. And once you experience this, once you taste the subtle flavors of afikomen, you won't want to taste anything else.

13. ***Barech***. *Birkat Hamazon*, the blessing recited at the end of the meal.

Life is a struggle, a burden, and often very painful. Above all, life is a blessing. The Hebrew word for blessing, *bracha*, is closely related to the word *breicha*, which is a free-flowing spring of water. Once we have grappled with our goals, striven to clarify our spiritual ambitions, and fought tooth and nail to master the conflict of body and soul, then we can view life with all the freshness of a clear, living stream.

A comfortably middle-aged couple from suburbia were visiting Israel for the first time. In Israel, all roads lead to Jerusalem. It was there that they struck up a conversation with an American who had recently settled in Jerusalem. They stood beneath the Western Wall and they talked. In the shadow of Jewish history yet unfolding, thoughts and feelings co-mingled as one. "What made you move to Israel?" They asked. "Israel," they were assured, "is a freshly prepared canvass; here you can touch your brush to the palette of life and use the colors of your soul and your history to paint your future and destiny."

That is the feeling of blessing. A canvass full of life and hope and promise just waiting to be painted. A sense of overwhelming potential and vibrant optimism, firmly rooted in reality while freely reaching for the stars.

14. *Hallel.*   The songs of praise.

> *My grandfather once helped someone who is now one of the most respected members of Congress break through what was then an almost impenetrable racial barrier. He gave him a job, an opportunity, and hope where society said he must not. He was tough, he was encouraging, and he was a friend. My grandfather is not with us anymore; but whenever given the opportunity, there is one man on Capitol Hill who continues to sing his praises.*

From the liberation in Egypt to the impossible rebirth of Israel, it sometimes seems that little has changed.

A Jewish cadet at West Point was taking a course on modern warfare. Korea, Vietnam, Afghanistan, Iran-Iraq the Falklands, and even the invasion of Grenada. Each was carefully analyzed for lessons which might be applied to future conflicts involving U.S. troops.

Well into the curriculum this cadet had a question. Why was it, he asked a commander, that not one battle involving Israel was ever studied? Not the Israeli War of Independence fought by a tankless, planeless "army" of hastily trained soldiers and Holocaust survivors against a well-armed invasion force; not the Six Day War, which Arab leaders promised would be the Jews' final dying breath; not the Yom Kippur War, which snatched near disaster from the jaws of one of histories largest sneak attacks; not a single one?

Could these glaring omissions be reflective of an anti-Semitic blind spot? Could Americans not stoop to learn how to fight from Jews? No, the cadet was assured, this was no ethnically derisive oversight — those wars just weren't normal. Those type of events, that type of fighting — the things that took place in all the battles that birthed and sheltered the Jews of Israel — just doesn't happen anywhere else. It doesn't pay to study them, because there is nothing for other countries to learn.

Tonight we feel the freedom of our history. Free of the historical strings which seem to bind all people to the predictable routes of nations and civilizations. Free of every societal force which attempts to restrict us to its path, its ideals.

Tonight we are free to be Jews. To be the Jewish people, and to make a difference. And free to sing the praises of One who broke the chains of bondage to set us free.

15. *Nirtzah*. Next year in Jerusalem — *L'shana Haba B'Yerushalayim.*

Every synagogue in the world faces Jerusalem. In prayer — whether in a synagogue, at home, or in an open meadow — every Jewish heart is directed towards Jerusalem. As the *ne'ilah* service draws to a close at the conclusion of Yom Kippur, congregations the world over proclaim, "Next year in Jerusalem." Every groom breaks a glass under the chuppah, and for a moment, all thoughts are on Jerusalem. And again tonight. In the waning moments of the Seder, every Jewish family prays — *Next year in Jerusalem.*

The name Jerusalem means "city of peace". Peace, *shalom*, is not merely the absence of conflict. Neither is it a utilitarian notion of cooperation and coexistence. Peace is the seamless harmony of individuals genuinely embracing a common vision. Not that each becomes lost in some faceless wave of the masses, but that each aspires to lend the beauty of his or her potential to the realization of a transcendent mission.

With *nirtzah*, with our eyes on the city of peace, we have come full circle. The pieces of our Passover puzzle are now in place. Where each had been part light, part penumbra, this vagueness has now given way to a brilliant singularity of vision. That our freedom be directed towards the imminence of Jerusalem — the imminence of peace.

Way back at *urechatz* we were transported to Jerusalem of old. It was then that we heard the words "*every goal must precede itself in thought.*" Jerusalem is our goal. That the wisdom and way of Jewish life should work to liberate the potential of every Jew, of the Jewish nation, and thus to transform the landscape of history. That somehow the intimate relationship of one lonely people to G-d should bear the fruits of spiritual symphony.

The fruit of freedom is peace. Peace of mind. Peace of body and soul. Peace within us, and so too, between us.

Next year in Jerusalem!

7

HOW TO USE THE
SURVIVAL KIT HAGGADAH

1. The Haggadah. It is a *mitzvah* — a commandment from the Torah — to *"speak about the exodus from Egypt"* at the Seder. This mitzvah is accomplished by reading and understanding the Haggadah. For this reason, the *Survival Kit Haggadah* includes an easy-to-read translation of the complete text of the Haggadah.

2. Commentary. In addition to reading and understanding the Haggadah, it is also vitally important to explore and discuss the meaning behind its words. The *Survival Kit* commentary allows you to take this important step. This commentary comes in two forms:

   A. Questions and answers. Questions are posed by either the wise, simple, or rebellious child. These questions are then answered in ways that go beyond the literal meaning of the text and explore deeper concepts and notions which are alluded to in the text.

B. Mini-essays. The *Survival Kit* often highlights and quotes a phrase or sentence from the Haggadah and then delves into its meaning and implications. Particular attention is paid to how these ideas are relevant to our lives today.

3. A suggestion. Take ten minutes before the Seder to familiarize yourself with the structure of this Haggadah. No two Haggadahs are arranged exactly alike, and the more familiar you are with the flow of the text — and how the commentary relates to the text — the smoother your reading will go.

The "official text" of the Haggadah always appears in a box with a thick black border around it. Everything outside of these text boxes is part of the commentary.

---

4. Blessings. All of the blessings which one is required to say at the Seder, i.e., for drinking wine or eating matzah, appear in Hebrew with both a transliteration and a translation.

5. **STOP** The stop sign indicates that it is time to fulfill one of the *mitzvot* (commandments) of the Seder, or to carry out one of the other observances. The *Survival Kit* provides general instructions on how to properly fulfill each mitzvah. Note: This is not a definitive book of Jewish law. There are good books available in English for anyone who wishes to pursue a more in-depth study of the laws of Passover.

6. **?** The question mark. This familiar symbol will appear throughout the Haggadah. Its purpose is to alert you to a question which may be appropriate to ask your guests — or yourself — at that point in the Seder.

7. Hashem. This word literally means "The Name" and is used in place of the conventional "Lord" to represent the name of G-d.

8. Relax and enjoy. Learn and grow.

8

THE SURVIVAL KIT HAGGADAH

KADESH (KIDDUSH)

STOP *The seder should begin, and kiddush should be recited, as soon after nightfall as possible. We wait until nighttime so that the entire seder takes place when it is actually Passover — which occurs with nightfall — yet we begin as early as feasible to facilitate the involvement of children.*

Kiddush is the first of the four cups. Each person's cup should be poured by someone else. This is how it's done for royalty, and tonight we are all members of a royal family.

On Friday night begin here:

And there was evening and there was morning,

The sixth day. The heaven and the earth were completed, and all that they contained. On the seventh day God completed His work which He had done, and He abstained on the seventh day from all His work which He had made. God blessed the seventh day and sanctified it; because on it He abstained from all His work which God created to make.

Kiddush begins here. On Friday night include words in parentheses.

Blessed are You, Hashem, our God, King of the universe, Who creates the fruit of the vine.

בָּרוּךְ אַתָּה יהוה אֱלֹהֵינוּ מֶלֶךְ הָעוֹלָם בּוֹרֵא פְּרִי הַגָּפֶן:

Baruch attah Adonai, eloheynu melech ha-olam, boray p'ri ha-gafen.

Blessed are You, Hashem, our God, King of the universe, Who has chosen us from all nations, who has exalted us above all tongues, and sanctified us with His commandments. And You, Hashem, our God, have given us in love (Shabbats, for rest), appointed times for gladness, feasts and seasons for joy, (this Shabbat and) this festival of Matzos, the time of our freedom (in love) a holy gathering to remember the Exodus from Egypt. For You have chosen us and sanctified us above all nations, (and the Shabbat) and Your holy festivals (in love and favor), in gladness and joy have You granted us our heritage. Blessed are You, Hashem, Who sanctifies (the Shabbat,) the Jewish People (Israel) the festive seasons.

Kiddush concludes with the following blessing.

Blessed are You, Hashem, our God King of the universe, Who has kept us alive, sustained us, and brought us to this specific time.

בָּרוּךְ אַתָּה יהוה אֱלֹהֵינוּ מֶלֶךְ הָעוֹלָם שֶׁהֶחֱיָנוּ וְקִיְּמָנוּ וְהִגִּיעָנוּ לַזְּמַן הַזֶּה:

Baruch attah Adonai, eloheynu melech ha-olam, she-he-he-yanu, ve-kiy'manu, ve-higi-anu la-z'man ha-zeh.

STOP *The wine should be drunk while leaning on the left side. It is preferable to drink the entire cup, but at the very least, one should drink most of the cup.*

URECHATZ (WASHING THE HANDS)

STOP *The procedure for washing one's hands is identical to when one washes before eating bread or matzah. Everyone except the leader of the seder should go to the kitchen. A large cup is filled with water. The water is poured twice on the right hand and twice on the left. Hands are dried, but no blessing is recited. Where possible; a cup, wash basin and towel should be brought to the table for the one leading the seder.*

KARPAS (VEGETABLE)

(STOP) Everyone should have a small piece of vegetable (celery or green pepper will suffice) which they will dip into salt-water. Before eating the vegetable a blessing is recited. This blessing not only relates to the karpas, but one should keep in mind that it also pertains to the maror, the bitter herbs, which will we be eaten later.

Blessed are You, Hashem, our God, King of the universe, who creates the fruit of the ground.

בָּרוּךְ אַתָּה יהוה אֱלֹהֵינוּ מֶלֶךְ הָעוֹלָם בּוֹרֵא פְּרִי הָאֲדָמָה:

Baruch attah Adonai, eloheynu melech ha-olam, boray p'ri ha-adamah.

YACHATZ (BREAK THE MATZAH)

(STOP) The leader of the seder breaks the middle matzah in half. The smaller piece is put back between the two remaining whole matzahs. The larger half is wrapped up to be used later as the afikomen.

MAGGID (THE HAGGADAH)

(STOP) The leader of the seder lifts the matzah for everyone to see and reads the following paragraph.

This is the bread of affliction that our forefathers ate in the land of Egypt. All who are hungry — come and eat. All those in need — come and celebrate Passover. Now we are here; next year may we be in the Land of Israel. Now we are slaves; next year may we be free.

This is the bread of affliction...

Simple Child: Why did the Jews eat matzah in Egypt?

Answer: Long before Manischewitz ever dreamt of egg, chocolate-covered, or whole wheat matzah, our Egyptian oppressors insisted that we subsist on matzah and little else. Matzah is more difficult to digest than bread, and though one may eat just a small quantity, the feeling of satiation lasts for a longer period of time. This enabled the Egyptians to reduce to a bare minimum the amount of wheat "wasted" on their slaves. The Egyptians also understood that a weakened body leads to a vulnerable spirit.

All who are hungry come and eat

After uncovering the matzah — symbol of our physical deprivation — we immediately turn our thoughts to the needs of others. The Pharaohs and Hitlers of history have made countless attempts to demoralize us by first crushing our bodies, hoping that our spirits would then be easy prey. But we will not be subdued. Right from the outset of the Seder we affirm our commitment to the maintenance of dignity despite all efforts to denude our hearts of human sentiment, our souls of their inclination to share.

Rebellious Child: *Now* we're inviting guests to the Seder! How insincere can you get? The Seder has already begun and there is no one around to invite!

Answer: Clearly the invitation to *"all who are hungry"* cannot be addressed to potential guests. Rather, we now lift our eyes from the Haggadah and address these words to those who are with us tonight. Sometimes, in our concern for people in far-off lands, we overlook the needs of those who are closest to us. At this point we reflect on our feelings for one another, for family, and for friends. It is time to let those who are right next to us know that their needs are important to us too — that we are concerned, that we care, and that we will always be there for them.

> This is a good time to think about what someone close to you needs, and how you can either assist or facilitate assistance. These needs can be physical, emotional, or spiritual.

Now we are slaves, next year...

Wise Child: What is meant by *"now we are slaves"* — in what way are we presently slaves?

Answer: In a society in which freedom reins and nothing is denied us, why do people seem to achieve so little of what they truly desire — a sense of accomplishment, peace of mind, and the feeling of fulfillment in life? Why is there such longing and groping, such squandered potential? Is it possible that we are yet slaves even in our freedom?

A person without a goal is certainly a slave to the vision of others. So we must ask — what are our goals? And then we must know that the price we pay to realize our lives' aims is the deliberate investment of immense effort. To live freely is a formidable challenge, and an uncomfortable one at that. A self-driven life is a long road strewn with potholes masquerading as rest areas. We had Walkmen, satellite dishes, and now the technology of virtual reality. Life's comforts are here to be enjoyed, but beware: for behind their friendly luster lays a scheme to enslave us all — to mollify our grit determination and to deny us our goals, our dreams, and ultimately our freedom.

Simple Child: I'm hungry, do we really have to read the whole Haggadah?

Answer: The reading of the Haggadah is far more than the telling of an overdone bedtime story. The reading of the Haggadah addresses itself to the innate human longing to know whence we came. Our present is profoundly linked to our past, and a murky notion of our origins will contribute to a sense of lonely detachment and inner estrangement. A child without a history is a child in search of place and purpose.

At the very least, and this is truly so very much, the Passover Seder confronts us with the responsibility of giving our children a sense of rootedness and belonging, of identity and direction. This Haggadah, we tell our children, this saga, is *your* saga. These events are your history, and these people are your people.

Likewise the ideas and values contained in the Haggadah are yours to consider. They are your inheritance, your family fortune.

The Haggadah tells us — as we tell our children — "You are a Jew." This is your past, your present, and the essence of your destiny.

> **?** Passover is a good time to think about ways in which you — or your family — can enhance your sense of Jewish identity. Is there something you can begin doing that will make being Jewish more meaningful?

> **STOP** *The Seder plate is removed from in front of the leader of the seder, and the second of four cups of wine is poured. It is customary for people to pour wine for one another. The youngest child then asks the four questions.*
>
> ### Mahnishtana: The Four Questions
> Why is this night different from all other nights?
>
> 1. **On all other nights** we eat chometz (leaven) and matzah, but on this night — only matzah.
> 2. **On all other nights** we eat various vegetables, but on this night — we eat bitter herbs.
> 3. **On all other nights** we do not dip even once, but on this night — we dip twice.
> 4. **On all other nights** we eat either sitting or reclining, but on this night — we all recline.

Mahnishtana — Why is this night different...

The *Mahnishtana* can actually be read in various ways. One can read it as four questions, as five questions, as one question with four examples or as one question with four answers. (Ask the people at your Seder how many questions they see contained in the *Mahnishtana*.)

Regardless of how one understands the *Mahnishtana,* it is

clearly calling our attention to a unique night. A nighttime, a period of darkness, unlike any other. And so we ask, why *is* this night different?

A friend and I drove from Cleveland to Denver. Truly we beheld a land of spacious skies, amber waves of grain, and majestic mountains. Nightfall was approaching as we passed through the heart of Kansas and within a few hours we were well into the Rocky Mountain state of Colorado. Denver was still quite a distance away, so we pulled off the darkened highway and slept by the side of a quiet road. With the sounds of morning and the first rays of sun we awoke to behold an unforgettable sight. Only a few hours earlier this same world had been shrouded in darkness. Now, as if from nowhere, great snow capped peaks surged valiantly towards the heavens. Awestruck, we reveled in a moment of singular beauty.

There is so much darkness in life. Dark cavernous voids that gnaw away at us. Darkness that clouds our vision of one another. Our ability to touch, to communicate, and to love. Darkness that pits us one against the other. Brother against brother, man against wife, nation against nation. And, in the dark of night, the Jewish nation was born. Surrounded by darkness while guided by the luminous rays of freedom.

Why is this night different? Because on this night we experienced our freedom. Why is this night different? Because only on this holiday do all the special observances, *mitzvot*, apply only at night. On Rosh Hashanah we blow the shofar only during the day. On Sukkot we sit in a Sukkah during the day or night. Only on Passover do so many *mitzvot* apply only at night. Why is this night different? Why is this the only night of the year so brimming with *mitzvot?* Because on the night of Passover we not only commemorate the moment of our birth, but we express the very meaning of our existence as a people. Our sages tell us, *"For the mitzvah is like a candle and the Torah a light."*

The purpose of Jewish existence is to be a source of light where otherwise darkness would hold sway. No matter how dark the world around us seems to grow, no matter how dim humankind's future may seem — the Jewish nation never gives up. Deep inside we all know that things can be different. Deep inside we feel the call to cast a light on a darkened life, or to illuminate a clouded corner of the globe.

At the foot of the Rockies the night's cool darkness told us, "There's nothing here." "Not so" said the light. "There is more than you can ever imagine."

Mahnishtana, why is this night different? Because dark as our lives may seem, lost though the world may have become, we still believe in the power of light. To illuminate our lives and our potential. To be a radiant force for all mankind. This is our message, and our goal. We will not rest until the dark night again shines like the day.

STOP *The seder plate is brought back, the matzahs remain uncovered and everyone reads and discusses the Haggadah.*

We were slaves to Pharaoh in Egypt, but Hashem our God took us out from there with a strong hand and an outstretched arm. And if God would not have taken our forefathers out from Egypt, then we, our children, and our children's children would still be enslaved to Pharaoh in Egypt. Even if we were all men of wisdom, understanding, experience, and knowledge of the Torah; there would still be a mitzvah for us to tell about the Exodus from Egypt. The more one tells about the Exodus, the more praiseworthy it is.

We were slaves to Pharaoh in Egypt

Rebellious Child: I'm sorry, but I have a hard time with a G-d who is strong enough to liberate the Jewish people from Egypt but allows them to become slaves in the first place.

> *Answer: No victory is as sweet as that of the once-vanquished, no freedom as empowering as that of the captive, and no light as luminous as one born in darkness.*

Without a doubt, no other people has endured what the Jews have been forced to endure. And, at the same time, *"I will insist that the Jews have done more to civilize men than any other nation. They have influenced the affairs of mankind more, and more happily than any other nation, ancient or modern."*[1] Think about it. When sworn enemies extend their hands in search of peace, are they not reaching for that noblest of human ideals contained in the Jewish message to humanity? That *"they shall beat their swords into plowshares [and] neither shall they learn war anymore."*[2] Yet no other people has been so utterly despised. *"Let us see what kind of peculiar creature the Jew is, which all the rulers and all the nations have together and separately abused and molested, oppressed and persecuted, trampled and butchered, burned and hanged"* — and now gassed. *"The Jew is the pioneer of liberty. The Jew is the pioneer of civilization. The Jew is the emblem of eternity."*[3]

On the one hand, Jewish history is a litany of mass abuse and human cruelty, while from another perspective; *"One way of summing up 4,000 years of Jewish history is to ask ourselves what would have happened to the human race if Abraham had not been a man of great sagacity and no specific Jewish people had come into being. Certainly the world without the Jews would have been a radically different place. Humanity might eventually have*

[1] John Adams, second U.S. President.
[2] Isaiah 2:4
[3] Leo Nikolaievitch Tolstoy. Russian author best known for *War and Peace* and *Anna Karenina*.

stumbled upon all the Jewish insights. But we cannot be sure. To them we owe the idea of equality before the law, both divine and human; of the sanctity of life and the dignity of the human person; of the individual conscience and so of personal redemption; of the collective conscience and so of social responsibility; of peace as an abstract ideal and love as the foundation of justice, and many other items which constitute the basic moral furniture of the human mind. **Without the Jews it might have been a much emptier place.***"[4]* (emphasis ours).

Over 2,000 years ago the prophet Isaih anticipated this twentieth century observation when he characterized the mandate of the Jewish people as being *"a light unto the nations."*

And why is there a need for such a nation? *"Because [people] had eliminated G-d from life, and even from nature, they found the basis of life in possessions and its aim in enjoyment."*[5] Or, more bluntly *"It is the duty for [each] man to live for his own sake, and not for others"*[6]

Therefore, *"it became necessary that one people be introduced into the ranks of the nations which, through its history and life, should declare that G-d is the only creative cause of existence. This mission required for its execution a nation poor in everything upon which the rest of mankind reared the edifice of its greatness and power; externally subordinate to the nations [who were] armed with proud self-sufficiency but fortified inwardly by direct reliance upon G-d, so that, by the suppression of every enemy force, G-d might reveal Himself directly as the sole Creator, Judge and Master of Jewish history."* [7]

The historical tapestry that is the odyssey of individuals, ideologies, and civilizations has but one constant. The Jew. Like the Soviet edifice of Marxism and the numbing specter of the Berlin Wall, empires from Rome to Britain have all crumbled

---

[4] Paul Johnson, *A History of the Jews* (New York: Harper and Row, 1987) p. 585.
[5] Samson Raphael Hirsch, *The Nineteen Letters* (New York: Fedlheim, 1969) p. 54.
[6] Fredrick Nietzsche, German philosopher and writer whose doctrine appealed to the Nazis.
[7] S.R. Hirsch, *The Nineteen Letters*, p.54.

while the Jew looked on. Somehow, in some inexplicable way, a tiny and undeservedly maligned people has succeeded — like historical yeast — in becoming a primary civilizing agent for mankind. Those nations, those self-appointed chieftains of history who would have eliminated the Jew have unknowingly become disciples of the very object of their ire.

The great span of our historical lifetime, like our birth in Egypt, is testimony to the fact that there exist no human or historical forces capable of overriding that which guarantees the impossible — Jewish survival. Survival with honor, with dignity, and with the mellow confidence of modesty.

The Haggadah is a portal to Jewish existential history. It wants us to ponder this question: Was it worth it? And it wants to know what you think. Not Adams, Tolstoy or Johnson, but you — what do you think? Was it — or more accurately, is it — worth the risk of being a Jew? It's Passover, and when your children ask, you better have an answer.

And if G-d would not have taken our forefathers out....

Wise Child: With all that has transpired in the world over the last 3,000 years, is it really conceivable that if G-d had not taken us out of Egypt that we would still be there today?

Answer: The enslavement mentioned in this section is an allusion to the multilayered meaning of slavery. And, just as slavery has connotations beyond physical bondage, so the reference to Egypt is more than just a geographic location.

While we would all like to think of ourselves as being perfect, fortunately, life often reminds us that we are not. As a result, when our car breaks down we call a mechanic, when our tooth hurts we visit the dentist, and when life aches we seek out one of the practitioners of therapy, recovery, or self-help with which our society is teeming. We all know that there are times when we need resources outside of ourselves who can assist us in identifying or solving a problem, charting a course, or achieving a goal.

The Hebrew word for Egypt, *Mitzrayim*, means constrain or stifle. A slave is certainly constrained and stifled. And aren't we all? Can't we all admit to ourselves that there are aspects of our lives which seem to be beyond our control — or anyone else's? That no matter how desperately we want something, we can't seem to discipline ourselves in ways that will facilitate achievement? That no matter how hard we try, we keep making the same mistakes over and over again? Well, how about this for a radical idea — ask G-d for help! It's not like He took early retirement after the exodus from Egypt, you know.

If the proverbial atheist in a foxhole will always turn to G-d for help, why can't we? Perhaps you could say that another way to translate *Mitzrayim* — is foxhole, and as we know, life is full of little foxholes.

> Note: When you go to a mechanic or doctor you are hardly "copingout." On the contrary, you are being mature, intelligent, and resourceful. Likewise with G-d. Judaism never advocates the abdication of responsibility to G-d, rather it submits that in our earnest efforts to achieve what we want, we often need help — even G-d's.

It once happened that Rabbi Eliezer, Rabbi Yehoshua, Rabbi Elazar ben Azaryah, Rabbi Akiva, and Rabbi Tarfon were reclining (at the Seder) in Bnei Brak. They were discussing the Exodus for the entire night, until their students came and said to them: "Our teachers, it is time to read the morning Shema."

Rabbi Elazar ben Azaryah said: I am like a seventy year old man, but I still could not succeed in having the Exodus from Egypt mentioned at night, until Ben Zoma expounded upon the verse which says: "In order that you may remember the day you left Egypt all the days of your life." The words "the days of your life" would have indicated only the days; the addition of the word 'all,' includes the nights as well. However, the other Sages teach that 'the days of your life' would mean only the world as we now know it; the addition of the word 'all' includes the era of the Messiah.

They were discussing the entire night

Time flies when you're having a good time. More than a hackneyed cliché, this adage is one that psychologists have actually studied and verified. The more meaningful, exciting, and interesting an activity, the faster time seems to go. And, as many veterans of the Seder trenches will testify, the opposite is also true.

Let your imagination loose for a moment and picture this: you have just concluded a marvelous encounter with the most adorable extraterrestrial you could ever hope to meet. A conversation transpired (though no words were actually spoken) and clearly your rendezvous was with a being of superior intelligence whose understanding penetrated the many layers of life and the universe. As a parting gift, you are left with a book, but there's one catch — in twenty-four hours it will mysteriously vanish. Now ask yourself: over those next twenty-four hours, how much time will you spend preparing and eating meals, watching television, or sleeping?

This is the Haggadah. A multilayered message about the meaning of Jewish existence, about life, and, most of all, about freedom. And all you've got is one night.

Remind your guests: anyone who finds a lesson about life, freedom, gratitude, or Jewish identity will receive a special prize — perhaps even an extra macaroon!

They were discussing...

Simple Child: Why were they discussing things all night when they should have been making a Seder?

> *"But I do love you," protested Dave. "Didn't I just buy you a beautiful sweater for your birthday, bring you flowers and serve you breakfast in bed?" "Yes, dear," came a loving if saddened voice, "but somehow I feel you were just going through the motions, that you're heart just wasn't there."*

Answer: Familiarity, complacency, and the routine of life — and even love — can chip away at the heart of any relationship. What remains is a shell; sometimes it cracks and sometimes it doesn't.

The same is true of spirituality. A spiritually vibrant life is the product of an ongoing commitment to developing an ever deeper relationship with the transcendental Creator. To achieve the intimacy of spiritual imminence, the Jewish people have in their possession a collection of specially designed tools. These are the *mitzvot*, or commandments, which work together to form a spirited mechanism for effecting an equable relationship between the limited and the limitless.

Like bouquets in a floral catalogue, each *mitzvah* is arranged to impart a particular message, meaning, and feeling. And all to enhance the relationship.

The Haggadah says that a group of rabbis in Bnai Brak were *"reclining."* This means that they were being careful to fulfill all the *mitzvot* of the Seder in the proscribed fashion of reclining.[*] They ate the matzah, drank the four cups, ate the meal, and read the Haggadah just as they were supposed to. And, at the same

---

[*] For more on reclining, see page (29)

time, they were intent on not allowing their actions — their fulfillment of the commandments — to become the stuff of brittle shells. Thus, *"they discussed the leaving of Egypt the entire night."* They spoke about the ongoing meaning and relevance of the exodus, about the purpose and message of the commandments of Passover, and, most importantly, about how it all fits together to nurture every Jew's relationship to G-d.

That the exodus from Egypt should be mentioned at night.

Life is full of little setbacks. Unexpected obstacles and unfriendly people or moods which seem to come from nowhere. An application rejected, a promotion denied, a senseless squabble with someone you love. Though none spells disaster, when taken together they become the *nights* of our lives. Painful, lonely, and even desperate.

So Ben Zoma gave us a tip about how to cope, and about freedom — even at night. *"That you may remember."* Remember the victories of your life. Remember those peak moments which gave you access to a higher state of consciousness. And, remember to keep things in perspective. That setbacks are setbacks, not tragedies. That problems are often opportunities in disguise — and never allow a few nights of darkness to overwhelm the beauty of life.

Recall your freedom, says Ben Zoma, even at night. Because a prison inmate who stubs his toe will limp his way out of work for a week — but if you stub your toe on the way out of Egypt, you just keep on running.

All the days of your life

Rebellious Child: Isn't this a bit obsessive? All day, all night, my whole life isn't it enough to remember the exodus on Passover and that will cover you for the year?

Answer: Remember the first baseball game your father took you to. The first time you told your husband you loved him, or the birth of your first child. There is something magical about first times in life. The impression they make on our souls is indelible, their resonant feelings are ever present.

Years later, when we find ourselves in need of inspiration, we can journey back to those magical firsts. Once again we can access that inventive state of mind, burst of creativity, or impulse to greatness. It is this journey in search of renewed inspiration to which Ben Zoma is directing us. Everyday when Jews recite the *Shema* and recall the exodus from Egypt, they attempt to return to that seminal moment of liberation. In so doing they strive to keep their commitments as vital and animate as the day they were born.

Blessed is the Place; blessed is He. Blessed is the One Who has given the Torah to His people Israel; blessed is He. The Torah is speaking to four sons: one who is wise, one who is rebellious, one who is simple, and one who does not know how to ask.

Blessed is The Place

There are those who will tell you that before the big bang got our universal ball rolling there was no time, space, matter, or energy. If this is true, as physicists and cosmologists insist it is, then the obvious question is: what *did* exist before our universe?

To figure that out all you have to do is close your eyes and see what appears when you rid your mind's eye of time, space, matter and energy. Go ahead — try it. Now, once you've made a few attempts, you will begin to realize that this visualization exercise is not only tough, it's impossible! Because if you could "see" what was there then obviously whatever you saw couldn't have been it. And even if all you saw was darkness, it had to be a darkness which filled a space, and remember — there was no space!

Are you scratching your head, wondering where the universe came from if what preceded it was absolute nothingness? Well, don't worry, the Haggadah has an answer to this puzzle of the universal antecedent. The Haggadah calls it *Hamakom*. The primordial Place.

Blessed is He

Wise Child: The main character in this little paragraph seems to be G-d, yet never once does the Haggadah use the name of G-d. It alludes to G-d with terms like "He" or "The Place," but why doesn't it just say G-d?

Answer: G-d's name has been obscured so that something else would be featured. Instead of highlighting G-d, here the Haggadah highlights *"that gave the Torah to His people Israel."* In Hebrew (as in English) the word for "gave" — *natan* — and the word for "gift" — *matanah* — are derived from the same root.

Consider this: what is the greatest gift you could give your children? Is it wealth, is it love, is it wisdom?

The Torah is not a history book. Neither is it law, ethics, or philosophy. The word *Torah*, in Hebrew, means instruction, and that's exactly what it is. Instructions for love and friendship, and for marriage and parenting. Instructions for personal freedom and spirituality, and for universal values and human understanding. Instructions for self-awareness, Jewish awareness, and the achievement of potential. As we say in our daily prayers — *Torat Chayim* — instructions for living.

If you could give your children the gift of sound wisdom and maturely cultivated counsel — wouldn't you? Well, G-d has the wisdom and the Torah is His gift.

> **?** 1. If you could only have one or the other — wisdom or wealth — which would you prefer?
> 2. What is the greatest gift parents can give their children?
> 3. Can wisdom be taught or must it come through experience?

The Torah is speaking to four sons

Rebellious Child: I'm vindicated! It says right here that the Torah is for kids and not for adults.

Answer: Very funny. The Torah was written for everyone: children, adults, and even people like you! Because a Jew is a Jew is a Jew, and like it or not, you are a part of us and we are a part of you.

There is an astonishing concept which says that every Jewish soul corresponds to a letter in the Torah. Each of us, in some mystical fashion, are woven into the timeless fabric of the Torah. We are each a part of the very essence of the Jewish people. So remember this: you can rebel all you want, but in the end you rebel only against yourself. Against your family, your people, and your very core. And make no mistake, while you can rebel even against yourself, you can never escape.

> This is a good time to remind everyone to be on the lookout for patterns of four appearing throughout the Haggadah.

Simple Child: I don't get it — is the Torah only for children?

Answer: The Torah is for everyone. Young or old, good or evil, educated or not. But in a way, to the Almighty, we are all children. In no other endeavor is the playing field so level, the rules so meritocratic, than in the human quest for a relationship with G-d. It doesn't matter who you are, where you've been, or what you have or haven't done in life. Like a loving parent, G-d is always there. Just go home and see for yourself.

One who is wise, one who is rebellious, one who...

Wise Child: We know that the number four is significant on Passover (see page 27), so there must be a reason why the word *one* appears four times in this paragraph.

Answer: Good observation — you get a prize. By attaching the word *one* to each of the four types of children, the Haggadah makes us focus on an attitude towards parenting which Judaism sees as being of paramount importance. King Solomon advises us to *"educate the child according to his way."* What this means is that every child is unique and must be related to in a way that befits his or her character. Our offspring are not mere replicas of ourselves, nor did they step off a page in the latest book on how to raise children. Moreover, there will never be another child who possesses the singular potential which we have been entrusted to nurture and polish.

Find that which is peerless in your child. Identify it, nourish it, praise it, love it, and most of all — speak to it. The Seder night: there is no better time to focus on your children then now. No better time for launching a tailor-made educational dialogue than tonight.

> **The wise son** — what does he say? 'What are the laws, statutes and ordinances which Hashem, our God, has commanded you?' Therefore you should explain to him the laws of the Passover Offering; namely, that nothing may be eaten after the afikomen — the final taste of the Passover Offering.
>
> **The rebellious son** — what does he say? 'What good is all this work to you?' He says, 'to you' and thereby excludes himself. And since he excludes himself from the Jewish people, this means he is denying God, the basic principle of Judaism. Therefore, you must blunt his teeth and tell him: 'It is because of this that Hashem did so for me when I went out of Egypt'. 'For me,' but not for him — had he been there, he would not have been redeemed.
>
> **The simple son** — what does he say? 'What is this?' Tell

him: 'With a strong hand did Hashem take us out of Egypt, from the house of bondage'.

As for the **son who doesn't know how to ask**, you must initiate for him, as it says, "You shall tell your son on that day: It is because of this that Hashem did so for me when I went out of Egypt."

Laws, statutes, and ordinances

When the wise son looks at Jewish life, he doesn't just see one monolithic mass of commandments; rather, he breaks them down into various types and categories. The wise son has honed his perceptive skills and has learned to draw distinctions. In fact, the ability to be thoughtfully discerning is one of the hallmarks of wisdom.

Each and every one of us is the object of intense competition. Not only do manufacturers and advertisers compete for our attention, but there exist a host of would-be peddlers of ideas and values who vie for our time and energy, our support and commitment, our votes — and, ultimately, our checkbooks.

Eventually everyone becomes a consumer. From the wise son we learn that one of the keys to freedom is becoming a thoughtful and discerning consumer, unless of course you don't mind being left with a bag of goods.

Nothing may be eaten after the afikomen

Wise Child: If you are supposed to teach the wise son *all the laws of Passover,* then why single out the laws of afikomen for specific mention?

Answer: Would Disney World be worth the trip if you had to come home empty-handed? No video, no photos, not even a postcard or T-shirt of Mickey? Perhaps in our rush to preserve every experience we have on some form of tape or film, we are in fact sacrificing a great deal. As we assume our position behind the camera and begin to stalk the big game of "Kodak moments," are we not also removing ourselves from the picture? Do we not become detached observers as well as active participants?

The law of the afikomen — namely, that once it's over — it's over, is a hint to the lost spiritual art of savoring. The art of savoring is a sensitization technique which allows us to become completely immersed in an experience. In Judaism this discipline of savoring, of emotional and intellectual relish, is essential to the path of personal growth known as *Mussar.*[*]

The Jewish art of savoring bids us to fine-tune our senses and to become more fully absorbed in both vision, sound, and their attendant feelings. In thought and ideas, as well as in internal impulses *and* their sources. To experience the dancing and the joy. The music, the tears, the love and the rarefied closeness they stir within us. To consciously engage every day and every moment; to celebrate life, and to imbibe the totality of every experiential step we take.

Upon concluding the Seder, Jewish law bids us not to taste anything after the afikomen. This is a night for savoring: ideas, feelings, and images. Parents teaching, children learning, and all of us growing together. Allow it to become a part of you. Savor this night of freedom. Only then can you leave. Not with souvenirs, not with photos, but as a different person. A different Jew. And this you will never forget.

> Choose one moment you want to remember from the Seder — close your eyes and savor it.

---

[*] *Mussar* is a branch of Jewish learning which explores the nuances of human personality, behavior, and character traits. It emphasizes personal growth and character refinement.

What are these laws, statutes, and ordinances

Rebellious Child: If this kid is so wise, how come he doesn't seem to know very much about all this stuff?

> *Freedom is power. Not the kind of corrosive power which can drive even the most genuine idealist to the brink of corruption, but the kind of power — or energy — which one derives from active participation in those decisions which affect the direction of our lives on a daily basis.*

Answer: Passover is *the time of our freedom,* and the wise son understands that the experience of the Seder is a precious opportunity which comes only once a year.

Inside each and every one of us lives a child of wisdom. We sense that there is more to Judaism than meets the eye. That what distinguishes a statute from an ordinance is more than just Jewish legal jargon, but rather a deeper set of ideas and spiritual constructs. That what separates one holiday from the next is not just the taste of seasonal delicacies, but distinctive opportunities for expanded consciousness. That under the rubric of Judaism is to be found something not only profound and insightful but deeply personal and meaningful.

Inside us all there is a voice that wants the privilege of a fully panoramic view of Judaism. To comprehend each facet of the Seder and how every nuance relates to the message of freedom, and the meaning of being a Jew. Listen to that voice. Refuse to sit there and just go through the motions. Be wise! Think, inquire and ask questions. Of Passover and its meaning for starters, and of Judaism and what it says about life as an encore.

Since he has excluded himself from the Jewish people, he has denied G-d.

During his freshman year of college, Sam had a part-time job as a census taker in a small town near the Ohio-Kentucky border. They wanted to open a liquor store in town and the state government required that there be a minimum number of residents in the area. Twice a week a group of student employees would go with a state worker to knock on doors and count heads. When the project ended the students eagerly awaited their paychecks — Sam's would finance a spring trip to Florida. You can imagine the shock when the state informed them that their checks would be delayed by a month or two.

Quite annoyed at the prospect of wishing his friends well as they departed for Ft. Lauderdale, Sam called the state worker who coordinated the group to express his feelings. "Meet me tomorrow at my bank" was his reply — and so he did. The next afternoon the state worker withdrew $500 from his personal account and handed it over to Sam. "When you receive a check from the state you'll pay me back," he said with confidence. "But why are you doing this?" Sam asked "Well," he answered, "you're Jewish, aren't you?" His question caught Sam off-guard. Then the man continued, "I am too, and that makes us brothers. Now don't tell anyone else about this and just send me the money when you get it." "Thanks," Sam said, and that was the last time they saw one another.

One of the little known phenomena related to the Six Day War is that Israeli consulates in the U.S. were besieged by volunteers eager to go to Israel and help. That Jews were ready to risk their lives is not so shocking; that many had names like Peterson, Smith and O'Donnell is. But they too were Jews — Jews who had shed every last vestige of identity and heritage in order to find a comfortable place among their neighbors. Yet there they were, Jews named Steinberg and Jews named Simpson, Jews named Cohen and Jews named Kelly — and when push came to shove — they all stood side by side as one family.

*   *   *

When Black Jews in Ethiopia are in trouble, Israeli soccer fans in Tel Aviv, doctors named Greenfield and Schwartz in St. Louis, and Jews speaking Portuguese on the beaches of Rio all respond. Over the last five years Israel has absorbed almost half a million immigrants, which is the proportional equivalent of the entire population of France suddenly relocating to the United States. To Israel's credit, with all the daunting social and economic strains this influx has placed on the country, never once has anyone of any political stripe even hinted that immigration should be slowed or halted.

*   *   *

What are we Jews anyway? Co-religionists, fellow nationals, compatriots — or — are we brothers and sisters? Born of one family and hewn of one stone? Are we bonded by a unifying relationship with G-d that is deeper than all which seems to divide us and render us strangers? And, could it be that when the rebellious son denies the quality of intrinsic Jewish connectedness, he not only turns his back on his brother, but on his Father as well?

You blunt his teeth... had he been there he would not have been redeemed

Listen carefully to the question of the rebellious child and see if you don't hear the voice of a child who is testing his limits — who wants to see just how much he can get away with.

To such a child we don't even offer an answer. Rather, we abruptly throw a vivid picture of the consequences of the direction he is taking right back in his face. *"Had you been there you would not have been redeemed!"* More than anything else the onus of his resultant destination may well serve as an effective educational means of forcing him to reconsider his ill-fated course.

Every Jewish child, and that includes us all, must be forced to consider this: Either you're with us or you're not; you can't have it both ways. Tonight, the choice is ours.

Simple Child: Why are you so mad at him? At least he's here — cousin Mitchell didn't even come.

Answer: Don't mistake our harshness for anger. We love this child as much as we love you and every one else at the Seder tonight. If we didn't care deeply about him we would have told him to take his cynical skepticism and go somewhere else for Passover — but we didn't. Intent as he may be on hurtling himself into the oblivion of a pseudo identity, we will always remain eager to teach him. We may have to say a few things that are painful for him as well as for us; but sometimes there is no choice.

No, we're not mad, but when it comes to cousin Mitchell — indeed — we are very, very sad.

What is this?

A simple question from a simple child.

> *"Yaacov (Jacob) was a simple man who dwelled in tents."* The Torah refers to our forefather Yaacov as a "simple man." At the same time our tradition has it that the *"tents"* in which our forefather Yaacov lived were the tents of wisdom. In Jewish consciousness Yaacov is the paradigm of someone who is wholeheartedly devoted to plumbing the depths of Torah for its full

bounty of wisdom. Strange — on the one
hand he was "simple," and on the other he is
the quintessential sage.

When your child asks you a simple question like, *"Why does a
magnet stick to metal?"* what are you going to say? Or how about
this one: *"Why doesn't it ever snow in the summer?"* Most of us
who are omniscient in the eyes of our children find ourselves
running for cover when these types of "cute" questions arise. *"I'll
be right back,"* we sheepishly assure them, as we are suddenly
reminded of an urgent call that has to be made. *"Why don't you
turn on the Discovery channel...?"*

You know why we don't have a lot of answers for our kids.
Because we did what we now secretly hope they will soon learn to
do — we stopped asking questions. What a tragedy. We have
sacrificed our youthful curiosity, our simplicity, if you will, on the
altar of intellectual sophistication.

Yaacov is characterized by our sages as the archetypical man
of truth. He was also a military strategist and a person of uncanny
insight into the nature of people and their personalities. A leader, a
visionary, and an idealist. A tower of wisdom, and of course, a
"simple man."

If you set your mind and your will to the task, you, too, could
earn a Ph.D. But will you be able to answer your children's most
pressing questions? Not "Why is the sky blue," but rather, "How
will I know if love is true?" Not "Why are there tears when people
cry," but "If no one is hurt, is it wrong to lie?"

Is it conceivable that the Torah revealed the truth of its wisdom
to Yaacov, not because he was the best and the brightest, but
because he was so simple. Could it be that if Yaacov, even with his
endowed intelligence, had stopped marveling at life's most
obvious questions, or had tempered his single-minded pursuit of
answers, that instead of being a wise man, he would only have
been a smart man? In the words of Albert Einstein, *"The most*

beautiful thing we can experience is the mysterious... He to whom this emotion is a stranger, who can no longer pause to wonder and stand rapt in awe, is as good as dead — his eyes are closed." Could it be that *"what is this?"* is not such a simple question after all?

?   If the wisest person in the world was at your Seder and you could only ask two questions — one about Judaism and one about life — what would those questions be?

What is this?

Rebellious Child: This kid isn't simple, he's stupid. What Jewish kid doesn't know what a Seder is, what matzah is, what macaroons are!

---

*T*he last time I saw my cousin she was twelve years old. She had accompanied her parents on a trip to Israel and was visiting my wife and me not long after we were married. She was bright, energetic, and possessed of a rare charm, still is, from what I hear. She's in college now and recently spent part of a summer working for my sister on a congressional campaign. Watching her carefree zeal my sister couldn't help but long, if only for a moment, for that rollicking spirit of freedom which animates collegiate life. I think about my cousin from time to time — and I wonder.

Her father is a therapist and an author. Her mother is an intellectual and an idealist. Both are deeply religious people and dedicated activists. Both are Protestant ministers. My cousin's mother, though born a Jew, had little formal connection with Judaism. My cousin has even less. I wonder — is she free?

Let my people go!

We act with a sense of urgency to free Jews in Russia, Syria, and Ethiopia. While on many fronts our efforts have met with success, there still exists another form of tyranny which must also incur the force of our wrath. This is the silent tyranny of ignorance. Ignorance, whether forced, induced, or knowingly chosen, is still ignorance. And if you don't know who you are then you are a slave.

My experience with Russian Jews tells me that when seated at a Seder table they will look at the matzah, charoset, and everything else and ask — *"What is this?"* I'm not so sure that those of us who had the privilege to be raised "in the land of the free" are really very different. Consider this: of the five and a half million Jews in America today, less than two million belong to synagogues. If most of them received a Jewish education, then at best maybe 30 percent of American Jews have ever learned about Judaism. Add to this the fact that most of these "educated" Jews finished their education at the age of twelve or thirteen; that one million American Jewish children are today being raised as non-Jews, or with no religion at all; and that another six hundred thousand Jewish adults are now practicing other religions, and what you've got is a tyranny of ignorance of immense proportions. What you've got is a silent Holocaust.

To date, over half a billion dollars has been spent to build Holocaust museums, memorials, and libraries in this country. While honorable monuments to the dead are being erected, the living are quietly exiting the stage of Jewish history.

"What is this?" is neither stupid or simple, but it may well be the last gasp for countless Jews.

The Russians can leave, the Ethiopians are home, there may yet be some semblance of peace in the Middle East, but it is still premature to lay down our arms and our cries for Jewish freedom. Because if you don't know who you are, you will never be truly free.

> ❓ How would you respond to a Russian Jew who says, "All my life I never had any religion and I was very happy; why should I start doing anything Jewish now?"

You must initiate for him

Ilya Essas grew up in a world where anti-Semitism was woven into the fabric of society. The word "JEW" was stamped on his identification papers and the penalty for teaching children about Judaism was three years in prison. Naturally, as a child, he learned very little about the Torah and his religion. Yet his parents taught him the one thing they well understood: it is an honor to be a Jew — you must always be proud of who you are.

Over the years this pride took on a life to its own. Not long after the Six Day War, Ilya and his wife Anya decided they wanted to emigrate to Israel. They wanted to go home. They put in a request for a visa, which was summarily rejected. At that moment their lives were changed forever. Now they were refuseniks. But this would not be the end of their dreams; instead it would be a beginning.

Eventually Ilya and Anya would become activists working on behalf of the refusenik community. In the process, Ilya would become a learned Jew. Illegal Jewish books (clearly subversive materials) became the staple of his intellectual diet. His sharp mind devoured text after text and with each one his commitment grew deeper and deeper. And then he went one step further. He became a teacher.

Ilya Essas became the driving force behind the underground network of Torah classes that eventually spread across the Soviet Union. A dynamic personality, he dreamt of rekindling a passion for

Judaism in the hearts of Russia's Jews. With large forums clearly out of the question, Ilya was forced to teach to small groups secretly gathered in peoples' apartments. Anyone who wanted could attend, with one provision. Whatever you learned, you had to promise to teach. Ilya Essas wanted not only students, he wanted revolutionaries. Modern-day Maccabees who were willing to risk everything to teach Torah and preserve Judaism.

Today the KGB, arch-antagonist of every refusenik, is a part of history. But Torah study is once again blossoming in Russia. And Ilya? They call him Rabbi Essas now, and he is still learning and teaching: in Israel.[*]

At this point the Haggadah reminds us of what we already know; that we are all responsible for one another. Whatever you know, you must teach; whatever you possess as a Jew, you must share. *"And you shall tell it to your son on that day."* At the moment when you stand face to face with a Jew who doesn't even know what to ask, then the responsibility becomes yours. Whether this is the child of a Russian or your own child, the child of your neighbor, or the child in the mirror.

You might think that the mitzvah to discuss the Exodus begins with the first day of the month of Nisan, but the Torah says: "You shall tell your son on that day." The expression 'on that day' could possibly mean only during the daytime; therefore the Torah adds: "It is because of this that Hashem did so for me when I went out of Egypt." The word this implies the presence of something tangible, thus 'You shall tell your son' applies only when matzah and maror are right in front of you — i.e. at the seder.

---

[*] For more on Ilya Essas see, *Silent Revolution: A Torah Network in the Soviet Union,* Miriam Stark Zakon, (New York, Mesorah Publications, 1992).

When matzah and maror are right in front of you

Matzah represents freedom and is contrasted with maror, which represents the bitterness of slavery. If the Haggadah may be appropriately subtitled *The Book of Freedom,* then the question being probed here is this: When is the best time for someone to learn about freedom? And to this query the reply comes: "When matzah [freedom] and maror [slavery] are *right in front of you.*"

- Work has been one frustration after another, and now your daughter wants you to teach her how to hit a softball.
- Your friends have an extra ticket to a concert, but you need the time to study.
- Someone just took your parking spot.
- Your husband looks like he's had a rough day, though you are convinced yours has been even rougher.

Being cognizant of our choices — of our capacity to control and direct our thoughts, feelings, words, actions, and reactions — is a prerequisite to freedom. These choices, some of them "big" but most of them not, are an ever-present reality. At all times they are quite literally *right in front of us*, and on some level each constitutes the choice between freedom and slavery.

Originally our forefathers were idol worshipers, but now God has brought us close to His service, as it says "And Joshua said to all the people, So says Hashem, God of Israel; your fathers lived on the other side of the river: Terach was the father of Avraham (Abraham) and Nachor, and they all served other gods. And then I took you father Avraham from the other side of the river and led him through the entire land of Canaan. I multiplied his offspring and gave him Isaac. To Isaac I gave Jacob and Esau; to Esau I gave Mount Seir to inherit, but Jacob and his children went down to Egypt."

From the other side of the river

Simple Child: When it says that Avraham (Abraham) was on the other side of the river, which river is it talking about?

Answer: The Haggadah doesn't mention this river by name because it's precise identity is irrelevant. What is relevant is the characterization of Avraham as being "on the other side." In fact, the name Avraham itself is derived from this very characterization. The Hebrew word for "other side" is *Aver*, and forms the root for the name Avraham.

When you travel to a different country, do you not feel the presence of a different spirit in the people and the culture? In looking back only a few years to the eighties or a few decades to the sixties, do you not sense that there was a different feeling in the air? A different mood and climate which in many ways distinguishes that time — and those people — from our time and us?

In many people's minds, each of us is essentially the product of the society in which we live. Values, morals, philosophy, religion, art, music — in short the totality of who we are — is but an expression of the time and place to which we belong. In the words of Hegel, *"Every individual is a child of its time [and] it is as silly to suppose that any philosophy goes beyond its contemporary world as that an individual can jump beyond his time"*

But "jump," nonetheless, is precisely what Avraham did. And, as his spiritual heirs, there is a bit of the jumper in each of us.

At the time of Avraham the entire world shared the same fundamental philosophy. The idea that reality consisted of gods of wind and fire was as self-evident to them as the force of gravity is to us. No one saw the world in any other terms, and it was impossible to view life from an alternative context, for none existed. Yet, there was Avraham. One man on one side of the river beckoning to an entire world on the other side.

The idea of one universal G-d, and all the ideals and values which follow from that reality are what the Jewish people have always stood for. Even when we were a lone voice; and even in the face of Auschwitz, the Gulag, and Madison Avenue. This is not only the legacy of Avraham, but freedom in its purest sense.

> Blessed is the One Who keeps His pledge to the Jewish people; blessed is He. For the Holy One, Blessed is He, calculated the end of the bondage in order to do as He said to our father Avraham at the Covenant Between the Pieces, as it says in the Torah; "He said to Abram, Know with certainty that your offspring will be strangers in a land not their own, they will enslave them and they will oppress them for four hundred years; but also upon the nation which they shall serve will I execute judgment, and afterwards they will leave with great wealth."

They will enslave them for four hundred years

Wise Child: If you calculate the number of years from the arrival of Jacob and his family in Egypt (2238BCE)until redemption (2448BCE), you come up with a total of 210 years — what happened to the other 190 years?

Answer #1

The Hebrew word for Egypt, *Mitzrayim*, means to be stifled or smothered. On a somewhat mystical plane we are told that those missing 190 years would eventually play themselves out during the future years of Jewish history and exile. The stifling presence of Egypt would be a nagging spiritual force that would hound the Jewish soul wherever it went. Perhaps it could be said that those 190 years were ground into tiny specks of timedust, metaphysical milliseconds, if you will. Then, scattered across the eons, these smothering particles of Egypt would work insidiously to suppress our ability — as individuals and as a nation — to scale the heights of spiritual potential.

But fear not. For just as the corporate glass ceiling can be pierced, so too this pernicious spiritual foe. Tonight, the Seder night, is known as *layl shimurim*, a night of shielding and security. The Seder is a spiritual refuge. A brief quietus during which the dust of Egypt is laid to rest. On this night of liberation we can see our struggles in a clear light. We not only see where we have been stifled, but can also detect a way out. Each Jew, and thus the collective soul of the Jewish nation, can eclipse that which dares to constrain us and begin to move on to new vistas of freedom.

> If there is an area of personal growth where you find yourself increasingly frustrated, perhaps you've even given-up, then now is the time to revisit that challenge. If you try, you should be able to tap a store of energy which you may never have detected before. And, what once seemed invincible may now become vulnerable to attack.

Answer #2

> *ebbetzin Kotler's devotion to Judaism and the Jewish people was such that she naturally became a model which others strove to emulate. Her profound love of Jews shaped every aspect of her life — even her diet.*
>
> *From the time of the Holocaust on, Rebettzin Kotler never once put anything sweet in her mouth. "Such tzores [so much pain] for the Jewish people how can I indulge in sweets?"* *

---

* For an article on the life of Rebbetzin Chana Kotler, see <u>The Jewish Observer</u>, May 1987.

When night after night Scud missiles were landing on Tel Aviv — each one a potential carrier of lethal gasses — how did you sleep? Comfortably, soundly, like one who hasn't a worry in the world? What Rebbetzin Kotler taught us is this: on such nights, Jews don't sleep. After all, what if your own children had been in Tel Aviv then?

Abraham and Sarah were told that their great-grandchildren were destined to be enslaved in Egypt. From the time their son Isaac was born until their grandson Jacob and his family were forced by a famine to seek refuge in Egypt, exactly 190 years had elapsed. Those missing 190 years of slavery could be found in the hearts of Abraham and Sarah. Each day they looked with the loving eyes of parents at their young son Isaac. Each day, in their mind's eye, and in their hearts, they would see the unspeakable horrors which Jewish children would suffer in Egypt. The 400 years of exile begin with the pain of Avraham and Sarah — exactly 190 years before the Jews went to Egypt.

Because Jewish joys belong to all Jews, and so do Jewish sorrows.

STOP *The matzahs are covered and the cups are lifted. Everyone reads the following paragraph with a feeling of joy. Upon its conclusion, the cups are put down and the matzahs are uncovered.*

And this is what has sustained our forefathers and us. For not only one has risen against us to destroy us, but in each and every generation they rise against us to annihilate us. But the Holy One, Blessed is He, rescues us from their hand.

"...in each and every generation..."

Simple Child: Have non-Jews really tried to destroy us in every generation?

Answer:

1430BCE — Slavery in Egypt.

356BCE— Achashverosh, King of Persia, decrees death to all Jewish subjects.

138BCE— Syrian-Greek government outlaws the practice of Judaism in Israel.

400CE— Saint John Chrysostom calls Jews "lustful, rapacious, greedy, perfidious bandits inveterate murderers."

486   — Monks and mobs burn synagogue, dig up a Jewish cemetery, and burn bones.

624   — Mohammed watches as 600 Jews are decapitated in Medina in one day.

640   — Jews expelled from Arabia.

1096   — First crusade: Thousands of Jews tortured and massacred.

1146   — Second crusade: Thousands of Jews, including women and babies, are butchered across Europe.

1200s— Jews "cause" the Black Plague. Jews murdered in Frankfort, Speyer, Koblenz, Mainz, Cracow, Alsace, Bonn, and other cities.

1290   — Jews expelled from England.

1306   — First expulsion of Jews from France.

1349   — Jews expelled from Hungary.

1391   — Spain: Seville, Majorca, Barcelona — tens of thousands killed.

1394   — Second expulsion from France.

1400's— Jews accused of murdering Christian children and baking matzah with the blood.

1421   — Jews expelled from Austria.

1492   — Jews expelled from Spain.

1496   — Jews expelled from Portugal

1500–1600s — The bones of Gracia de Orta, a Jewish scientist and "convert" to Christianity, are exhumed and burnt because he was a Marrano (secret Jew). Elsewhere, Marranos are burned in Mexico, Portugal, Peru, and Spain.

1553 — The Talmud is burned in Italy.

1648–66 — Cossacks, Poles, Russians, and Swedes massacre Jews.

1744 — Jews expelled from Bohemia and Moravia.

1818 — Pogroms in Yemen.

1840 — Blood libel in Damascus.

1862 — General Ulysses S. Grant expels Jews from Tennessee.

1882 — Pogroms in Russia.

1930s–40s — Official Canadian reply to most Jewish pleas for refuge: "Unfortunately, though we greatly sympathize with your circumstance, at present you cannot be admitted. Please try some other country." (Of course, there were no other countries; only the gates of Auschwitz remained open.)

1939–45 — Six million Jews are annihilated across Europe. Babies serve as target practice, women are human guinea pigs for doctors and scientists, beards are torn from men's faces.

1948–67 — Fearing for their lives, Jews flee Algeria, Iraq, Syria, Yemen, Egypt.

1917–91 — The study of Hebrew is a "crime against the state" in the Soviet Union.

1992–94 — Committee for Open Debate on the Holocaust runs full-page ads in university newspapers across the U.S. claiming that the Holocaust never took place.

1993 — Anti-Jewish publications sell briskly in Japan. A leading Japanese newspaper carries an ad which reveals a Jewish plot to weaken and enslave Japan.

...in each and every generation

Wise Child: If we understood the reasons for anti-Semitism, couldn't we begin to eliminate it?

Answer: During the summer of 1993 Steven Spielberg was on site in Poland filming "Schindler's List." Today, of over 3 million Jews who lived in Poland prior to World War II, barely 10,000 remain. The present population of Poland is 32 million, which means that in a Super Bowl crowd of 90,000 you would find about 30 Jews.

When members of Spielberg's cast and crew mixed with local Polish residents, they were shocked to find themselves confronted with open expressions of a visceral hatred for Jews. The Poles have taught us an astonishing fact: the fire of Jew hatred requires no fuel. Like some horrific alien, it is able to feed off its own flesh.

"Our forefathers and us... in each and every generation."

Teachers are experts at discerning the difference between excuses and reasons. Protestations of "but I left my assignment in my locker last night" often fall on deaf ears. Because after all, couldn't a conscientious student easily have called a friend for the assignment? Thus, reasons are quickly unmasked for the hollow excuses they truly are.

Ten reasons why non-Jews have hated Jews:

1. They are different from us.
2. They are wealthy.
3. They are not loyal citizens.
4. They are too involved in the government.
5. They kill non-Jewish children and use their blood in the baking of matzah.
6. They invented the G-d of moral conscience.
7. They are poor and parasitic.
8. They are becoming too much like us.
9. They killed G-d.
10. They want to rule the world.

Virtually every item on this list is contradicted by another. The question is this: Are there any legitimate reasons for Jew-hatred, or are there only excuses? A) What do you think? and B) Is there any way to counter the persistence of Jew-hatred?

In each and every generation

Simple / Wise/ Rebellious Child: How have we survived such an onslaught?

Answer: There is a dimension of Jewish thought known as *gematria*, or numerology. This approach to Jewish learning attaches a numerical value to every letter in the Hebrew alphabet. In accordance with a strict set of rules, scholars are often able to reveal hidden meanings by uncovering ideas that are numerically encoded in various words and sentences. The Haggadah says, *"And **this** is what has sustained our forefathers and us..."* The Hebrew word for *"this"* is *v'hē*, which is a four letter word consisting of a *vav, the* sixth letter of the alphabet, a *hey*, the fifth letter, a *yud*, the tenth letter, and an *aleph*, the first letter.

Perhaps these four letters are an allusion to the source of our national endurance.

- *Vav* = 6 — corresponds to the six sections of the Talmud, the Oral Torah.*
- *Hey* = 5 — is the five books of the Written Torah.
- *Yud* = 10 — is the Ten Commandments.
- *Aleph* = 1 — as in "G-d is one."

Through it all, Jews have always seen themselves as having a profound relationship with the transcendental G-d who is One. A vibrant observance of the commandments, coupled with an unfailing dedication to studying the wisdom of the Torah, is both the expression of that relationship and the force which has propelled us through time.

---

* Note: The classical view of Torah is that it was communicated to Moses on Mt. Sinai in two parts. Firstly a written text, and secondly a complementary oral elaboration which served to elucidate the written text. This oral text was eventually written down in the form of the Talmud.

> | ? | If you remove these elements, what else is there to being Jewish? |

Go and learn what Laban the Aramean tried to do to our father Yaacov (Jacob). Though Pharaoh's decree was only against the males, Laban attempted to uproot and destroy everything, as it says in the Torah; "An Aramean tried to destroy my father. Then he (Yaacov) descended to Egypt with a small family and sojourned there; and there he became a nation — great, powerful, and numerous."

Then he (Yaacov) descended to Egypt — forced by a decree of God.

Sojourned there — this teaches that our father Yaacov did not intend to settle in Egypt, rather to reside there on a temporary basis, as it says; "They (the sons of Yaacov) said to Pharaoh: "We have come to sojourn in this land because there is no pasture for the flocks of your servants, because the famine is severe in the land of Canaan. And now, please let your servants dwell in the land of Goshen."

With a small family — as it says; "With seventy soul(s), your forefathers descended to Egypt, and now Hashem, your God, has made you as numerous as the stars of heaven."

Forced by a decree of G-d

We all know, though we are often loathe to admit it, that greatness in life is forged in the face of adversity. Somehow it is those formative life experiences which come as the blow from a sculptor's hammer and chisel — and not the painter's soft strokes — upon which we reflect with the deepest sense of satisfaction. Great mothers are molded more by the difficulties they encounter raising their children then by the times when their little ones behave like "perfect angels." We comfort and empathize with those who have suffered, while we revere those who triumph in the face of disaster.

*T*oday in Jerusalem there lives a master teacher by the name of Avraham. If they learn nothing else, every student he meets learns — at the very least — to have a greater appreciation for life, and to see almost all their troubles as trivial. No small lessons indeed.

I had the privilege to study in a yeshiva with Avraham and was once invited to spend the holiday of Sukkot with him and his wife. He celebrated the holiday and lived life just like anyone else — despite being paralyzed from the neck down. He insists that the day of his accident was the most important day of his life. Now he has a keener appreciation of the meaning of life and the blessing of what it means to "just" be alive.

As I said, he is a teacher and motivator of unparalleled excellence. You simply can't meet him and not be changed by the encounter.

No, we never wish accidents, illness, or even flat tires, missed appointments or stained ties on anyone. Yet we know that the trials of life, both great and small, are where superior quality of character and living are ultimately fashioned.

"Forced by the decree of G-d..." We often have little control over the circumstances of our lives and the situations with which we are confronted. There is divine orchestration in life. Our role — our shot at freedom — is to address the conditions of our lives and to respond to all that comes our way with the type of dignity, maturity, and courage that makes us better human beings for having passed that way.

Yaacov did not intend to settle in Egypt, rather to reside there on a temporary basis...

Have you ever felt that your goals and inner aspirations were somehow at odds with the values espoused by the popular culture surrounding you? You want to be a successful human being, while social context impels you towards a successful career. You are grappling with spiritual concerns and an attempt to map out a "road less traveled," while society shunts such matters off to the fringes of public and private life alike. A clandestine tug-of-war ensues, leaving you feeling like a refugee in your own home. Your choices seem so polar — to drown in the undertow of the milieu, or to be different.

Jacob knew that part of the path to greatness is to consciously remain an outsider. And though greatness may at times be a lonely goal, and leadership a solitary position, he saw that the lot of the outsider was intrinsic to the success of the Jewish people. To be a *"light unto the nations"* is to be prepared for difference. To be consciously out of step with popular ideas — and if need be — to remain that way.

As seventy soul(s) your forefathers

Wise Child: It says here that the Jews went down to Egypt *"as seventy soul"*, shouldn't it say "seventy souls" in the plural form instead of the singular?

Answer: The singular use of the word "soul" points us to another essential quality which allowed the Jewish people to flourish in the monstrous pit of Egypt. In so doing, it also sheds some light on the dynamics of spiritual attainment.

> *About a week before the beginning of every holiday I receive a phone call. And every time a familiar voice asks the same question, — "How's it going?" This is not the automated "How's it going" of perfunctory social graces; this guy really means it. You see, he's a friend. A comrade in arms. Someone who is pledged to my success — and I to his — as we attempt to root our dreamy idealism in the*

reality of life. And so he wants to know "How's it going?" — which should be read as "Have you given the opportunity inherent in the upcoming holiday any thought yet? Are you searching for new insights, new shots at growth, new ways to find inspiration?"

*   *   *

Most friendships just kind of happen. A chance meeting on the golf course, a college roommate, kids in the same class. Conversation develops, common interests emerge, paths begin to cross more often, and before you know it — you're friends.

That friend who calls me before the holidays? We *chose* to become friends. In many ways our personalities are night and day. Our assets and liabilities of character are the mirror image of one another. Our minds don't often think alike and we tend to look at things differently. So why did we choose to become friends? Because we share common life goals. Like each of you, we both want to live as meaningful a life as we can. To make growth a synonym for life, and rather than mark time, to fill it.

And for this one needs a friend. Because although we all have lofty ambitions, we dare not mention such matters too loudly, lest they be held up as a model against the way we actually live. We fear the accusation, if only by a faint inner voice, of being hypocrites. Of advocating one set of values and goals while pursuing quite another. Precisely for this reason we need to carefully choose our friendships. For while you can dodge a faint inner voice, you can't dodge the eyes — or voice — of a friend.

*   *   *

Now imagine a community whose primary point of relationship is a common vow to the same aspirations and objectives. To the spiritual aim of transforming the mundane into the meaningful, and the routine into inspiration.

This was the family of Jacob — the nascent Jewish nation —

which *"descended"* into the abyss of Egypt. Each with his or her own personality and perspective, each with a distinctive nature and style. Strikingly individual, yet possessed of a common "soul" which drew them together into a striving, caring, and nonjudgmental community.

In describing the Egyptians, our sages tell us that their cruelty was only surpassed by an unfettered addiction to everything lewd and degrading. At the same time we are told that *chesed,* the trait of sensitive sharing and thoughtful assistance, was an aspect of Jewish life which never weakened in Egypt. That we were redeemed from bondage was one miracle, that any trace of humanity and spirituality remained was quite another.

Surely this was a portent of things to come. A people forced to endure not only the most heinous physical abuses but the simultaneous crushing force of a world that seeks to rob us of character, integrity, and sanity itself. There is only one road to survival. As one soul. Insisting upon our mandated right to strive for everything that lifts our hearts and inspires our souls.

> **?** Are you aware of the life goals of your friends, spouse, or children? Do you consider yourself to be a part of a community? If so, what unites that community?

There he became a nation — this teaches that the Jews were a distinctive people there.

Great, powerful — as it says; "And the children of Israel were fruitful, increased greatly, multiplied, and became very, very powerful; and the land (of Egypt) was filled with them."

Numerous — as it says; "I made you as numerous as the plants of the field; you grew and prospered, and became charming, beautiful of figure; your hair was long; but, you were naked and bare. And I passed over you and saw you downtrodden in your own blood, and I said to you: Through your blood you will live. And I said to you: Through your blood you will live."

And the Egyptians did evil to us and afflicted us; and imposed hard labor upon us.

The Egyptians did evil to us — as it says; "Let us deal wisely with them lest they multiply and, if we should to be at war, they might well join our enemies and fight against us and then leave the country."

... the Jews were a distinctive people there

Rebellious Child: If Jews are forced to wear distinctive clothes or a yellow badge, that's one thing; but why in the world would we *choose* to be distinctive? Wouldn't it make a lot more sense to just blend in? That's what I plan to do.

In 1987, when the collapse of Communism and the fall of the Berlin Wall still seemed decades away, a rabbi named Shalom went to meet with refuseniks in the Soviet Union. When he returned, the look in his eyes was enough to tell you that what he encountered there had been truly profound. He spoke about Soviet Jews who risked everything just to be Jewish. To study Hebrew, learn Torah, and to emigrate to Israel. Many of his initial contacts were made at train stations or on crowded streets where they were less likely to fall under the watchful eye of the KGB.

"But in the midst of a crowd, how could you identify a refusenik you had never met?" someone asked. "Simple," was Shalom's reply. "Refuseniks are the only people in Russia who smile."

Answer: Our tradition has it that the Jews in Egypt were conspicuous in three ways. By the style of their dress, by the language they spoke, and through their use of Jewish names. Additionally, our sages tell us that the Jews of Egypt made a pact. No matter how desperate their situation became, they would continue to emulate their forefather Abraham and act towards one another with kindness and compassion.

No matter how self-centered the society around them, and no matter how hard it tried to corrupt their spirits, the Jewish people were determined to remain distinctive.

Like the 500 families of the Litzmannstadt Ghetto who opened their homes to orphaned children, the Jewish people would be kind amidst the most hellish brutality; tender and gentle in a world of steel-cold hearts.

In Egypt, Jews were different on the outside as an ever-present reminder that they were also different on the inside. Not long ago Jewish children in Kiev defied the KGB every time they listened to someone read a Chanukah story. Somehow I have a feeling that in Egypt of long ago — as in the Soviet Empire of our time — Jews wore a distinctive smile.

Great, powerful...

My daughter likes to roll up her sleeve, snap her arm into position, and challenge anyone within earshot: "Feel my muscle."

But what about us? Those of us who grapple with an interminable expansion of waistline, and who have traded in our war-torn jogging shoes for a more sedate pair of Air Walkers — what evidence can we produce that we too are the proprietors of enviable strength?

True strength is inner strength. To admit that you've made a mistake — that takes strength. To stand with a friend while others stand by laughing — that takes strength. To deal honestly where deception would be more lucrative — now that takes strength. The strength which was cultivated in Egypt was the strength of inner convictions.

> **?** Have you made any recent decisions or pursued a course of action which contributed to the development of your private muscles of inner tenacity?

And the Egyptians did evil to us...

In Hebrew the words *"did evil to us"* can also be read as *"they made us see ourselves as evil."*

As the literature on parenting will tell you, "labeling is disabling." Convince a child that he or she is a "bad" boy or girl, and you will have succeeded at thwarting much of their ability to grow into the human being they could have been.

The Egyptians may have been depraved, but they weren't stupid. They sought out ways — *"let us deal wisely"* — to cast Jewish values in a disparaging light. Where we might see selfless dedication to the needs of others as noble acts, the Egyptians would see only a burdensome denial of self. Where we would see the existence of a transcendent G-d, they saw the humorous folly of empty devotion.

Slavery, the capitulation of our convictions to the expediency of social conformity, often begins with subtle self-doubt. At every turn we hear the voice of the Egyptians:

- "Don't be silly..."
- "No one believes *that* anymore..."
- "Would you get with it already..."
- "You don't want to be like *them* do you?"
- "You're not serious, are you?"

With time, the impact of these voices begins to take its toll. They cast a lifeless shadow over the bright light of our lives. They label us — and we become disabled.

And Afflicted us — as it says; "They set taskmasters over them in order to oppress them with their burdens; and they built the treasure cities of Pithom and Ramses for Pharaoh."

They imposed hard labor upon us — as it says; "The Egyptians enslaved the children of Israel with brutal labor."

We cried out to Hashem, the God of our forefathers; and Hashem heard our voice and saw our affliction, our burden, and our oppression (Deuteronomy 26:7).

We cried out to Hashem, the God of our forefathers — as it says; "It happened over those many days that the king of Egypt died; and the children of Israel groaned because of the work and they cried out in anguish; and the crying caused by the work rose up to God."

Hashem heard our voice — as it says; "God heard the groaning, and God recalled His covenant with Avraham, with Yitzchak (Isaac) and with Yaacov."

And saw our affliction — this refers to the disruption of family life, as it says; "God saw the children of Israel and God was imminently aware."

Our burden — refers to the children, as it says; "Every son that is born you must throw into the river, but every daughter you will let live."

Our oppression — this refers to the pressure, as indicated by the words, "I have also seen how the Egyptians are applying pressure upon them."

The treasure cities of Pithom and Ramses

Simple Child: Was building these two cities the only work of the Jewish slaves?

Answer: Our need for meaning may be second only to our need for air. It is so basic that even the existentialist who sees existence as nothing more than an anxiety- riddled fluke, is forced to come up with some sort of meaning with which to pad the dreary cell of life. It is so powerful that an entire branch of psychoanalytic thought* rests on the assertion that when one is deprived of meaning, all is lost, yet given a sense of meaning, one can prevail over the worst suffering and deprivation.

Believe me, Pharaoh knew exactly what he was doing. The Talmud relates that the region of Pithom and Ramses was a wet, sandy marshland hardly fit for a construction site. But Pharaoh's real aim was destruction, not construction. He chose the site of Pithom and Ramses because he hoped that the futility of Jewish efforts would give rise to a sense of inescapable anguish. (Like being a sports fan in Cleveland.) Each morning the Jews were once again saddled with the fate of fruitless labors. Brick after meaningless brick, their hollow feeling of agony intensified.

Part of the responsibility of freedom is the obligation to fill our lives with meaning. And, in a world filled with a thousand follies masquerading as life's most cherished activities, that responsibility weighs particularly heavy.

In a gas-filled room a horrified human being will still desperately gasp for air. And when all else fails, the season-long saga of ones favorite team will just have to do.

? Would you risk losing your home, or your arm or your life, for any of the following?
A. Bringing famine relief to millions of starving people.
B. Being the MVP quarterback of a Super Bowl champion.
C. Bringing peace to Northern Ireland.
D. How about to the Middle East?
E. Finding a cure for cancer.
F. Winning an academy award.

This refers to the pressure

We're under a lot of pressure. Just look at people, or yourself,

---

* The school of logotherapy was originated by Dr. Victor E. Frankl, author of *Man's Search for Meaning*.

and see if it doesn't seem that some indomitable boss is standing over us all, making sure that every minute is a busy minute.

According to the eighteenth-century philosopher and mystic Rabbi Moshe Chaim Luzzatto, there actually is such a boss. And this boss, this hovering prince of pressure, is symbolized by none other than Pharaoh himself. The embodiment of everything oppressive.

Rabbi Luzzatto speaks of a force which seeks to wreak internal havoc simply by never giving us a moment's rest. For if given time to rest and reflect, Pharaoh knows that his days as a slave driver would soon be over. Pharaoh's arch-enemy, the champion of freedom, is quiet contemplation.

> **?** When was the last time you took a good chunk of time to think about questions like: What are my priorities? Am I concentrating on the things I really ought to be? Is there any way to creatively restructure my time?

Hashem brought us out of Egypt with a strong hand and with an outstretched arm, with great awe, with signs and with wonders (Deuteronomy 26:8).

Hashem brought us out of Egypt — not through an angel, not through a special angel, not through a representative, rather God Himself, in his glory, as it says; "I will pass through the land of Egypt on that night; I will slay every firstborn in the land of Egypt, from man to animal; and upon all the Gods of Egypt will I execute judgments; I, Hashem."

"I will pass through the land of Egypt on that night" — I and no angel; 'I will slay every firstborn in the land of Egypt' — I and no special angel; "And upon all the gods of Egypt will I execute judgments" — I and no representative; "I Hashem" — I and no other.

With a strong hand — this is the pestilence, as it says; "The hand of Hashem will smite your cattle which are in the field, the horses, the donkeys, the camels, the herds, and the flocks — it will be a very severe pestilence."

With an outstretched arm — refers to the sword, as it says; "And His sword is drawn in his hand, it is outstretched over Jerusalem."

With great awe — alludes to the obvious fact of God's direct involvement, as it says; "Has God ever attempted to take for Himself one nation from the midst of another nation; by trials, signs, and wonders, by war, with a strong hand, an outstretched arm and by awesome means; just like Hashem your God did for you in Egypt, before your very own eyes?"

With signs — refers to the staff, as it says; "Take this staff in your hand, so that you may perform the signs with it."

With wonders — this is the blood, as it says; "I will display wonders in the heavens and on the earth."

Not through a representative, rather G-d Himself

Wise Child: If there are no forces that are independent of G-d, then isn't everything ultimately done through G-d Himself and not a representative?

Answer: Yes, but think of it this way. Just like a successful business owner may delegate many of the tasks necessary for the smooth running of his business to others, there remain certain jobs which just can't be delegated — ever. When it comes to human history, the survival of the Jewish people is one such job. And, over the course of our long exile, it's nice to know who is ultimately in charge.

One nation from the midst of another...

This quote is taken from a section in the Torah (Deuteronomy 4:25–40) in which Moses is delivering his parting speech to the Jewish nation just prior to his death. At that moment Moses tells of a future epoch, when *"G-d will scatter you amongst the nations and you will be there a tiny minority."* In his prophetic words Moses goes on to explain that one of the results of this long exile will be a profound estrangement of Jews from a relationship to G-d and Judaism. We will seek meaning and spirituality in every sort of religion, ideology, and "ism." And then Moses turns his vision, and his words, to the Jewish people living in that distant future. He knows that having been set adrift on the rough waters of history that we will begin to seek the shelter of truth. But how will we know? How will we be able to know if our very own Judaism contains an authentic path to achieving a bond with G-d?

To know this, Moses says, speaking to these searching Jews of the future, *"Please investigate world history back to its earliest times, and see if an event of this magnitude has ever taken place or if such an event has ever been heard of."* And what is this unique historical event which Moses is referring to? *"Has an entire nation ever heard G-d speak or has G-d ever brought one nation out from amidst another nation as G-d has done for you in Egypt?"*

In quoting these words of Moses, the Haggadah gives us the essence of what makes Judaism unique. Judaism, and only Judaism, claims to be rooted in a national historical event experienced by an entire nation. The intellectual bedrock of Jewish belief never rests on one man's claim to divinity or revelation, nor that of a small band of witnesses. Jewish commitment to Judaism is ultimately rooted in the idea that while national historical events may be open to reinterpretation, they can never be either fabricated or erased. The Vietnam War, like the Kennedy assassination, will be debated for years to come. But there is one idea that will never take hold, namely, that these events never happened at all. No conspiracy theory is big enough to invent events of such national consequence in which so many people were involved. Similarly, though the leaders of the Soviet Union would paint Stalin in a variety of shades from savior to demon, there are two things they could never do. Deny him or invent him. The national events which had Stalin at their helm were simply too big to hide and too far reaching to have been fabricated.

But Moses went even one step further. Consider his words carefully: "if an event of this magnitude has ever taken place *or if such an event has ever been heard of.*"

Over 3,000 years ago Moses predicted the unpredictable. When he prophesied that no such event would *"ever be heard of,"* what he was saying was this: though the Jewish people will always stake it's spiritual claim in the soil of historicity, no other people or religion will ever even attempt to do the same. And historical hindsight bears out this confident vision of Moses. For in fact, no other religion has ever attempted to mount the stage of world history by staking it's claim on the veracity of a national historic event.

And just how did Moses know that this would be the case? The answer is this. Though dreams, visions, and personal revelations can easily be claimed by any individual or committee seeking to found a religion, you just can't claim that a national historical event happened if it didn't. It just won't fly.

Moses knew prophetically what logic likewise dictates. If the Jews were smart enough to come up with a story of national redemption and revelation, then eventually some other group would also invent its own equally compelling story. But we didn't, and they couldn't.[*]

On the night of Passover Jewish parents don't tell bedtime stories, they teach history.

Take this staff in your hand...

Wise Child: Why did G-d tell Moses to hold a staff before initiating the plagues?

---

[*] NOTE: This idea is not meant to stand on its own as a rational for Jewish belief. It is but one piece of a much larger picture which deserves careful thought and consideration.

Answer: One of the most serious impediments to bringing one's potential to fruition is what Judaism calls *ya'ush* — utter despair. The doleful lament of one who sees inescapable limitations and recurrent failings as proof positive that all the future holds is the drudgery of survival at best, or bitter failure at worst. *Ya'ush* sets in when one finally accepts that he or she will never achieve anything of great significance, or will never "amount to anything."

The message of the staff is one that calls on us to bravely standup to *ya'ush* — to despairing of one's abilities and potential — and to boldly insist that our lives are still ours to live.

On the surface, the staff of Moses was nothing more than a piece of dead wood. We can almost hear ourselves saying, "there is about as much chance of me changing myself, let alone the world, as there is of a stick being able to turn a river into blood." But that is exactly what happened.

The staff urges us to look beneath the surface. To detect the hidden rumblings of potential where there seems to be none. In ourselves as well as in others. In children, students, friends, spouses, and even in the Jewish people. Leave no stone unturned in the search for hidden strengths and capabilities. Discover them, value them, and carefully nurture them. And know — each in our own unique way — we *can* make a difference. We can accomplish and contribute, and above all, we can override the clutches of despair and once again begin to grow.

STOP *As each of the following words; blood, fire, and smoke, is said, a bit of wine is removed from the cup, either with the finger or by pouring.*

Blood — Fire — And Pillars of Smoke

An alternative explanation of the preceding verse says that each phrase represents two plagues. Mighty hand — two; outstretched arm — two; great awe — two; signs — two;

wonders — two. These correspond to the ten plagues which the Holy One, Blessed is He, brought upon the Egyptians in Egypt, namely:

STOP *As each of the plagues is mentioned, a bit of wine is removed from the cup. This is repeated for each word of Rabbi Yehudah's Hebrew abbreviation.*

1. Blood 2. Frogs 3. Lice 4. Wild Beasts 5. Pestilence 6. Boils 7. Hail 8. Locusts 9. Darkness 10. Death of the firstborn.

Rabbi Judah abbreviated them by using a mnemonic comprised of the first Hebrew letter of each plague.

D'TZACH	**ADASH**	**B'ACHAB**
(1,2,3)	(4,5,6)	(7,8,9,10)

STOP *The cups are refilled with fresh wine to replace what was removed.*

PHARAOH AND THE TEN PLAGUES:
A Three-Part Story

Part I: Setting the Scene

Simple Child: Why didn't Pharaoh and the Egyptians let the Jews go after one or two plagues? I sure would have.

Answer: The story of the ten plagues is recorded in the Torah in the book of Exodus, 7:8–12:33. There the Torah reports that the Egyptian court magicians were able to duplicate the first two plagues. For this reason Pharaoh was convinced that he was facing a force with which he could at least contend. However, the great philosopher, grammarian, and biblical commentator Rabbi Avraham Ibn Ezra (1089–1164) explains that a close reading of the text reveals that in truth the Egyptian magicians were no match for Moses and his brother Aaron. In fact, the best the Egyptians could do was to turn a small bottle of water into blood. They certainly couldn't transform the mighty Nile into a bloody waterway. Yet despite these feeble attempts to duplicate the plagues Pharaoh contented himself with these meager displays. Pharaoh continued to cling to his conviction not to free the Jews despite Moses' warning of even more dire consequences. As you may recall, there is a little bit of Pharaoh in us all.

Part II: Rationalization Reaches for Straws

Life is a battle. We all want to do what's right and good, but it's such a struggle. And, when locked in this pitched battle we often give in to our impulse towards rationalization. Rationalization affords us a respite, as it enables us to justify actions which deep down we know are not for us. This remarkable ability, when viewed from a distance, would often be laughable if it weren't so destructive. Like Pharaoh and his magicians, we often hang our hats on the crudest line of thinking in order to sanction that which flies in the face of who we are and what we want to stand for. And if we are not vigilantly self-aware, then we run the risk of sharing Pharaoh's fate. In the grips of rationalization, Pharaoh the slave master became Pharaoh the enslaved. Clinging to straws, we seek to excuse some actions and justify others, while hurtling unchecked towards our own self-destruction.

Part III: The Tunnel Vision of Ego

You consider a course of action, carefully weigh all the options and permutations, and finally arrive at a conclusion. Your decision has been made and you're off and running. At first the going is smooth, but soon you find that you keep stubbing a toe. Then you twist an ankle, injure a knee, throw out your back, and eventually run face-first into a brick wall which everyone saw but you.

Dazed and bruised you ponder a most ancient riddle: "Where

did that come from?" The answer may well lie in the fact that the only thing harder than admitting you've made a mistake is running headlong into the consequences. Such was Pharaoh and such is life.

To admit that the sum total of all our careful calculations and detailed planning is nothing more than a brilliantly charted course to failure is simply too much to bear. Our egos just won't allow us to hear of such nonsense. So we don a pair of designer blinders sporting the Pharaoh logo and rush off into the grasp of everything we wanted to avoid. Or, unlike Pharaoh, we can refuse to ever shut our eyes and have the courage to sacrifice our egos before we sacrifice ourselves.

Rabbi Yossi the Galilean said: From where do we learn that the Egyptians were struck with ten plagues in Egypt, but with fifty plagues at the Sea? Regarding the plagues in Egypt the Torah says; "The magicians said to Pharaoh, It is the finger of God."However when it comes to the sea, the Torah says; "Israel saw the great hand which Hashem laid upon the Egyptians, the people feared Hashem, and they believed in Hashem and in His servant Moses." How many plagues struck them with the finger? Ten. So we can calculate that if they were struck by ten plagues in Egypt (where the instrument was a finger), they must have been struck by fifty plagues at the sea (where the instrument was a whole hand).

Rabbi Eliezer said: From where do we learn that every plague that the Holy One, Blessed is He, inflicted upon the Egyptians in Egypt was equal to four plagues? Because it says; "He sent upon them His fierce anger [in the form of] **wrath, fury, trouble** and **emissaries of evil**. Each plague in Egypt contained four elements; 1) **wrath,** 2) **fury,** 3) **trouble** and 4) **emissaries of evil;**" therefore we can calculate that in Egypt they were struck by forty plagues and at the sea by two hundred plagues.

Rabbi Akiva said: From where do we learn that each plague that the Holy One, Blessed is He, inflicted upon the Egyptians in Egypt was the equivalent of five plagues? Because it says: "He sent upon them His **terrible anger, wrath, fury, trouble,** and **emissaries of evil.**" Each plague in Egypt thus contained five elements; 1) **terrible anger,** 2) **wrath,** 3) **fury,** 4) **trouble** and 5) **emissaries of evil,** therefore we can calculate that in Egypt they were struck by fifty plagues, and at the sea by two hundred and fifty plagues.

Ten plagues... forty plagues... two hundred and fifty plagues...

Rebellious Child: Who cares how many plagues there were? G-d did a bunch of miracles to free the Jews and that's all we need to know.

Answer: At the conclusion of a delicious dinner when a child says, "thanks mom," before running outside, or when his father says, "thank you dear," before grabbing the paper, the question is this: how thankful are those guys anyway?

A sincere expression of gratitude draws both benefactor and provider closer together. Every couple should know that a vivid recollection of kindness bestowed is a powerful way to draw two hearts together.

Think about all the effort that goes into the average dinner. It begins with someone thinking about which foods will be both nutritious and tasty. This is followed by a look in the fridge to check what ingredients are not on hand, the composition of a shopping list, and the drive (at times in the nastiest of weather) to the grocery store.

After numerous trips up and down the aisles — searching for just the right ingredients at just the right price — there follows the trip home, which ends with shlepping in the heavy bags and putting everything away. All this precedes various types of preparation — from boiling water to dicing vegetables, the cooking, and then the clean-up.

From this bird's-eye view we can begin to see that the list of kindnesses and efforts involved in many of the daily deeds from which we benefit — and tend to take for granted — is remarkably long.

The more carefully you consider each aspect of what someone does for you, the closer and more connected you will feel. Earnest gratitude will draw your heart close: to your parents, your spouse, and to the Almighty as well.

Now is a good time to say thank you. Some suggestions:

1. To the person, or people, who worked so hard to prepare the Seder. Have everyone at the table say thank you for a specific aspect of the Seder which they appreciated.

2. Ask everyone to thank G-d for one blessing in their life. This can be shared or said privately.

3. Ask people to thank a family member for something they did in the past which may have gone unrecognized.

The Omnipresent God has bestowed an abundance of favors upon us!

Had He brought us out of Egypt,
but not executed judgments against the Egyptians
   Dayenu -this would have been enough.
Had He executed judgments against them,
but not upon their gods,
   Dayenu -this would have been enough.
Had He executed judgments against their gods,
but not slain their firstborn,
   Dayenu -this would have been enough.
Had He slain the firstborn,
but not given us their wealth,
   Dayenu -this would have been enough.
Had He given us their wealth,
but not split the sea for us,
   Dayenu -this would have been enough.
Had He split the sea for us,
but not led us through it on dry land,
   Dayenu -this would have been enough.
Had He led us through it on dry land,
but not drowned our oppressors in it,
   Dayenu -this would have been enough.
Had He drowned our oppressors in it,
but not provided for our needs in the desert
for forty years,
   Dayenu -this would have been enough.
Had He provided for our needs in the desert
for forty years,
but not fed us the Manna,
   Dayenu -this would have been enough.
Had He fed us the Manna,
but not given us the Shabbat,
   Dayenu -this would have been enough.
Had He given us the Shabbat,

but not brought us before Mount Sinai,
   Dayenu -this would have been enough.
Had He brought us before Mount Sinai,
but not given us the Torah,
   Dayenu -this would have been enough.
Had He given us the Torah,
but not brought us into the Land of Israel,
   Dayenu -this would have been enough.
Had he brought us into the Land of Israel,
but not built the Temple for us,
   Dayenu -this would have been enough.

Certainly, how much more so, should we be thankful to the Omnipresent for all the favors He did for us: He brought us out of Egypt; executed judgments against the Egyptians; as well as their gods; slew their firstborn; gave us their wealth; split the sea for us; led us through it on dry land; drowned our oppressors in it; provided for our needs in the desert for forty years; fed us the Manna; gave us the Shabbat; brought us before Mount Sinai; gave us the Torah; brought us to the Land of Israel; and built us the Temple to atone for all our transgressions.

DAYENU — ENOUGH

Vision, Balance, and Growth

The Jewish approach to living is growth-oriented. Judaism, like a loving if demanding parent, is forever encouraging us to go one step further. To transcend our present selves and to soar higher and higher. This outlook on life is the expression of an eternally optimistic and confident view of human beings. At the same time, it contains a treacherous pitfall. If the driving force in life is to continually grow, improve, and better oneself, then this can tend to breed a concurrent feeling of inadequacy and even failure. What good, after all, are my accomplishments if I can always — must always — be driven to surpass them?

It is to this dilemma that the two-sided coin of *Dayenu* directs our attention. In the first instance *Dayenu* isolates each and every step from the redemption in Egypt until the Jewish people finally enter the land of Israel and build the Temple in Jerusalem. Here, *Dayenu* is suggesting that with each one of these progressive steps we stop and say — enough! Not that we lower our sights or rest on our laurels, but that we celebrate each individual accomplishment as an enriching experience of growth. To appreciate that a significant step has been taken and to feel it's inherent pleasure. Yes, we can always deepen our relationship with G-d, but we must also know that each new level of depth forever changes who we are. True, we could always be kinder and more empathetic, but we need to be aware that every compassionate gesture makes an indelible impression on our soul and psyche.

This is the view from the first half of *Dayenu*. Then comes the flip side. Here we recognize that G-d was not satisfied with leaving us at any one of these steps of experiential growth, and that ultimately we had to travel the full distance from Egypt to Jerusalem. Therein lies a picture of our own determination. To lift our eyes and gaze out at that which resides in the realm of the dreamer. As impossible as it was for the oppressed slave in Egypt to imagine the splendor of the Temple in Jerusalem; as impossible as it was for a Polish Jew locked in a cattle car bound for hell to envisage today's Israel, is how impossible it often seems that we will ever rise above our failings to realize our innermost dreams.

DAYENU — If our sights are always set on the most distant shore. *DAYENU* — If we relish every moment of growth. Then *DAYENU* — there is no limit to what we can achieve, and no end to the pleasure we will experience with each new stride we take.

Rabbi Gamliel used to say; Whoever has not discussed the following three things on Passover has not fulfilled his obligation, namely: **Pesach** (the Passover Offering); **Matzah; Maror** (the Bitter Herbs).

Pesach — Why did our forefathers eat the Passover Offering during the period when the Temple still stood? Because the Holy One, Blessed is He, passed-over the houses of our forefathers in Egypt, as it says; "You shall say: It is a Passover Offering for Hashem, Who passed over the houses of the children of Israel in Egypt when he struck the Egyptians; as for our houses — they were spared; and the people bowed down and prostrated themselves."

🛑 *The leader of the seder lifts the middle matzah for all to see while the following paragraph is recited.*

Matzah — Why do we eat it? Because the dough of our forefathers did not have time to become leavened before the King of Kings, the Holy One, Blessed is He, revealed Himself to them and redeemed them, as it says; "They baked the dough which they had brought out of Egypt into matzah for it had not fermented; this was because they were driven out of Egypt and could not wait; also, they had no other provisions prepared."

🛑 *The maror is lifted for everyone to see while the following paragraph is recited.*

Maror — Why do we eat bitter herbs? Because the Egyptians embittered the lives of our forefathers in Egypt, as it says; "They embittered their lives with difficult labor, with mortar and bricks, with all sorts of jobs in the field; whatever labor they made them perform was excruciating."

In each and every generation each individual must see himself as though he personally had gone out of Egypt, as it says; "You shall tell your son on that day: It was because of this that

> Hashem did for **me** when I went out of Egypt. It was not only our forefathers whom the Holy One redeemed; we, too, were redeemed with them, as it says; He brought **us** out from there so that He could take us to the land which He had promised to our forefathers."

Pesach, Matzah and Maror [*]

Each individual must see himself...

This statement identifies a central, though elusive, goal of the entire Seder experience. Namely, that on Passover every Jew is to tingle with emotion as he or she rejoins the Jewish people at the original moment of redemption.

And just how is it that we — traveling through life with computers on our laps and phones in our cars — can hope to realistically achieve this experiential sensation of leaving Egypt?

The key to this dilemma is two-fold. It is a mix of the painstaking, down-to-earth personal growth to which Passover calls us, with an almost mystical encounter with the ever-present soul of the Jewish people. In fact, this very paragraph hints to the existence of this two-fold approach to a timeless convergence of past and present.

The first half of this paragraph speaks to us in the singular. *"A person... you should tell your son... G-d did for me,"* while the second half is in the plural. *"Not only our forefathers... we too were redeemed... in order to bring us."*

This subtlety of language points to the two planes upon which we are to experience the freedom of Passover. As our hearts and minds engage the entirety of the Seder, we are both dynamically autonomous individuals as well as molecular bits of the aggregate soul of the Jewish people.

---

[*]For a fuller discussion on these ideas refer to the following pages in the *Passover Survival Kit:* Pesach (25) Matzah (69) Maror (69).

As individuals, we wrestle with Egypt for our personal freedom. We initiate the type of introspection in which we identify our essential goals, our arch impediments, and necessary strategies for actualization. Without goals, freedom is an elusive tease. Without an awareness of entrenched deterrents, it's a fantasy. And without thoughtful generalship, it just won't happen.

Superimposed onto our personal strivings for freedom is our souls' linking up with an eternal spiritual dimension of existence known as *Klal Yisroel*, the Jewish people. It is to this that our consciousness is drawn when the Haggadah speaks to us in the plural. *"Not only our forefathers did G-d redeem, but **we too** were redeemed with them."*

My body dies a million deaths as its cells silently decay and become mingled with the dust of history. Though most of the original me is long gone, *I* remain. The essence of self is a constant.

A '67 Chevy, though rebuilt from fender to fender, is still a '67 Chevy. And the same *Klal Yisroel*, the same Jewish nation which experienced the exodus from Egypt, is still alive today.

Tonight our personal quest for freedom, and the part of us that was present at the exodus, are fused together as one. And it is just this fusion which creates the potential to see ourselves as if we personally left Egypt.

STOP *The matzahs are covered and the cup is lifted and held while the next three paragraphs are read.*

Therefore we must thank, praise, pay tribute, glorify, exalt, honor, bless, extol, and acclaim He Who performed all these miracles for our forefathers and for us. He brought us from slavery to freedom, from sorrow to joy, from mourning to celebration, from darkness to abundant light, and from enslavement to redemption. Let us, therefore, utter a new song before Him! Halleluyah!

Halleluyah. Praise, you servants of Hashem, praise the Name of Hashem. May the Name of Hashem be blessed, now and forever. From the rising of the sun until its setting, Hashem's Name is praised. Above all nations is Hashem, above the heavens is His glory. Who is like Hashem, our God; He Who is enthroned on high; Who lowers Himself to look at heaven and earth. He raises the destitute from the dust, from the trash heaps He lifts the needy - to seat them with the nobility, with the nobles of His nation. He transforms the barren wife into a joyous mother of children. Halleluyah.

When Israel went out of Egypt, the house of Jacob from an alien people; Judah became His sanctuary, Israel His dominion. The sea saw and fled; the Jordan turned back. The mountains skipped like rams, the hills like young lambs. Why o' sea do you flee? O Jordan, why do you turn back? Mountains, why do you skip like rams; hills like young lambs? The earth trembles before the master; before the God of Jacob; The One who turns the rock into a pond of water, the flint into a flowing fountain.

Who lowers Himself to look at the heaven and the earth

The "heaven and the earth" are the spiritual and the physical. The lofty and the commonplace.

G-d is not an elitist who keeps company only with the upper-crust of the spiritually attuned, or who will only be seen at the most select of venues. G-d considers every aspect of every life to be of supreme value; from the most sublime moments of meditation and prayer, to the mundanity of eating and conjugal intimacy. Thus, in the eyes of a Jew, all moments are but vessels of potential waiting to be filled with value, with spirituality, and with meaning.

STOP *The cup is lifted and the matzahs covered during the recitation of this blessing.*

Blessed are You, Hashem our God, King of the universe, Who redeemed us and redeemed our ancestors from Egypt, and allowed us to arrive at this night so that we could eat matzah and maror. Therefore, Hashem, our God and God of our forefathers, enable us to experience future holidays and festivals in peace, joyful in the rebuilding of Your city, and happy in Your service. There we will eat of the sacrifices and the Passover Offerings, whose blood will be upon the sides of Your altar and be acceptable. In your honor we will compose a new song which celebrates our redemption and our spiritual liberation. Blessed are You, Hashem, Who has redeemed Israel.

Blessed are You, Hashem, our God, King of the universe, Who creates the fruit of the vine.

בָּרוּךְ אַתָּה יהוה אֱלֹהֵינוּ מֶלֶךְ הָעוֹלָם בּוֹרֵא פְּרִי הַגָּפֶן:

Baruch attah Adonai, eloheynu melech ha-olam, boray p'ri ha-gafen.

STOP *After the blessing everyone drinks the second cup of wine. 1) Be careful not to speak after the blessing until the cup has been drunk. 2) Lean to the left while drinking. 3) Try to drink the entire cup, or at least most of it.*

RACHTZAH (WASHING THE HANDS)

STOP *The procedure for washing is identical to the washing done earlier at urechatz. However, this washing will be followed by two blessings, and one should try not to speak from the time of the blessing until after eating the matzah. Everyone except the leader of the seder goes to the kitchen. A large cup is filled with water which is poured twice on the right hand and twice on the left. The rachtzah blessing is recited, hands are dried, and everyone returns to the table to recite the next two blessings before eating the matzah. When possible, the leader of the seder should wash at the table.*

Blessed are You, Hashem, our God, King of the universe, who has sanctified us with His commandments, and commanded us with the washing of the hands.

בָּרוּךְ אַתָּה יהוה אֱלֹהֵינוּ מֶלֶךְ הָעוֹלָם אֲשֶׁר קִדְּשָׁנוּ בְּמִצְוֹתָיו וְצִוָּנוּ עַל נְטִילַת יָדָיִם:

Baruch attah Adonai, eloheynu melech ha-olam, asher kid-shanu b'mitzvo-tav, ve-tzivanu al ne-tilat yada-yim.

MOTZI

STOP *At this point we fulfill the mitzvah to eat matzah on the night of Passover. Each person should have two thirds of a piece of matzah on their plate; half a piece is sufficient if hand baked matzahs are used.*

The leader of the seder lifts all three matzahs from the seder plate and recites the following blessing.

Blessed are You, Hashem, our God, King of the universe, who brings forth bread from the ground.

בָּרוּךְ אַתָּה יהוה אֱלֹהֵינוּ מֶלֶךְ הָעוֹלָם הַמּוֹצִיא לֶחֶם מִן הָאָרֶץ:

Baruch attah Adonai, eloheynu melech ha-olam, ha-motzi lechem min ha-aretz.

STOP *The bottom matzah is put down, and the following blessing is recited while the top (whole) matzah, and the middle (broken) piece are still raised.*

MATZAH

STOP *The bottom matzah is placed back on the seder plate before reciting the next blessing. Following this blessing everyone should eat their piece of matzah while reclining on the left side. One should keep in mind that this blessing also relates to the korech-sandwich and the afikomen which will be eaten later.*

Blessed are You, Hashem, our God, King of the universe, who has sanctified us with his commandments, and has commanded us with the eating of matzah.

בָּרוּךְ אַתָּה יהוה אֱלֹהֵינוּ מֶלֶךְ הָעוֹלָם אֲשֶׁר קִדְּשָׁנוּ בְּמִצְוֹתָיו וְצִוָּנוּ עַל אֲכִילַת מַצָּה:

Baruch attah Adonai, eloheynu melech ha-olam, asher kid-shanu b'mitzvo-tav, ve-tzivanu al achilat matzah.

MAROR (BITTER HERBS)

🛑 *The leader of the seder dips a large piece of maror into charoset, and then shakes off the charoset. One such piece is given to each person. The following blessing also relates to the maror eaten with the korech-sandwich. After reciting the blessing everyone eats the maror **without** reclining.*

Blessed are You, Hashem, our God, King of the universe, who has sanctified us with his commandments, and commanded us with the eating of maror.

בָּרוּךְ אַתָּה יהוה אֱלֹהֵינוּ מֶלֶךְ הָעוֹלָם אֲשֶׁר קִדְּשָׁנוּ בְּמִצְוֹתָיו

וְצִוָּנוּ עַל אֲכִילַת מָרוֹר:

Baruch attah Adonai, eloheynu melech ha-olam, asher kid-shanu b'mitzvo-tav, ve-tzivanu al achilat maror.

KORECH (SANDWICH)

🛑 *The korech-sandwich is made as follows: using one-third of a piece of matzah, and a large piece of maror which is dipped in charoset (the charoset is shaken off), one makes a sandwich which is eaten after saying the following paragraph. The sandwich is eaten while reclining to the left.*

As a remembrance of the Temple we now do as Hillel did in the time of the Temple. He would combine the Passover Offering, matzah, and maror in a sandwich and eat them together. This is a fulfillment of what it says in the Torah; "They shall eat it (the Passover Offering) with matzahs and bitter herbs."

SHULCHAN ORECH (THE MEAL)

🛑 *What everyone has been waiting for. The festive Passover meal. While one should enjoy the Passover dinner, it is important to leave room for the afikomen.*

TZAFON (AFIKOMEN)

STOP *Using the afikomen, and additional matzah as needed, each person receives two-thirds of a piece of matzah: half a piece is sufficient if hand-baked matzah is used. The afikomen should be eaten while leaning to the left.*

BARECH (BLESSING AFTER DINNER)

STOP *At this time, before Birkat Hamazon (the blessing after meals) the third cup of wine is poured. It is customary for people to fill one another's cup.*

Birkat Hamazon

Blessed are You, Hashem, our God, King of the universe, Who nourishes the whole world; in His goodness, with favor, with loving-kindness, and with compassion. He gives sustanance to all flesh, for His loving-kindness is eternal. And because of His great goodness we have never lacked food, and may it never be lacking to us forever. For the sake of His Great Name, because He is the God Who nourishes and sustains all beings, and does good to all of them, and He prepares food for all of His creatures which He has created. Blessed are You, Hashem, Who provides food for all.

We thank You, Hashem, our God, because You have given to our forefathers as a heritage a desirable, good and spacious land; because You brought us forth, Hashem, our God, from the land of Egypt and You delivered us from the house of bondage; for Your covenant which You sealed in our flesh; and for Your Torah which You taught us, and for Your statutes which You made known to us; for life, favor, and loving-kindness which You granted us; and for the food with which You feed and sustain us constantly, every day, in every season, and in every hour.

For all this, Hashem, our God, we thank You and bless You. May Your Name be blessed continuously and forever by the mouth of all living things. As it is written, 'And you shall eat and be satisfied and bless Hashem, your God, for the good land which He gave you.' Blessed are You, Hashem, for the land and for the food.

Have compassion Hashem, our God, on Israel Your people, on Jerusalem Your city, on Zion the resting place of Your Glory, on the kingdom of the house of David, Your anointed, and on the great and holy House upon which Your Name is proclaimed. Our God, our father – tend us, feed us, sustain us, nourish us, relieve us; Hashem, our God, grant us speedy relief from all our troubles. Please, Hashem, our God, left us not be needful of the gifts of human hands, nor of their loans –but only of Your Hand; that is full, open, holy, and generous, that we not feel shame or humiliation – forever and ever.

On Shabbat add the following paragraph:

May it please You, Hashem, our God – fortify us through Your commandments and through the commandment relating to the seventh day, this great and holy Shabbat. For this day is great and holy before You, to observe the Shabbat on it and be rest on it in love, as commanded by Your will. May it be Your will, Hashem, our God, that there be no distress, no grief, or sighing on this day of our rest. And show us, Hashem, our God, the consolation of Zion, Your city, and the rebuilding of Jerusalem, city of Your holiness, for You are the Master of salvations and Master of consolations.

Our God and God of our fathers, may there arise, come, reach, appear, be accepted, be heard, be counted, and be remembered before You – the remembrance of ourselves, the remembrance of our fathers; the remembrance of the Messiah, the son of David, Your servant; the remembrance of Jerusalem, Your holy city; and the remembrance of Your entire people, the House of Israel, before you. For survival, for well-being, for favor, for loving-kindness, and for compassion, for life and for peace on this day of the Festival of Matzos. Remember us on it, Hashem, our God, for goodness, count us on it for blessing, and deliver us on it for life. Regarding salvation and compassion, have pity, show favor and be compassionate upon us and help us. For our eyes are turned to You; for You are the Almighty King, gracious, and merciful.

Rebuild Jerusalem, the Holy City, speedily in our days. Blessed are You, Hashem, Who rebuilds Jerusalem. Amen.

Blessed are You, Hashem our God, King of the universe, the Almighty, our Father, our King, our Mighty One, our Creator, our Redeemer, our Maker, our Holy One, Holy One of Jacob, our Shepherd, the Shepherd of Israel, the King who Is good and beneficent to all beings For every single day He did good, does good, and will do good to us. He has rewarded us, is rewarding us, and will forever reward us – with favor and with loving-kindness and with compassion, with relief, salvation, success, blessing, help, consolation, sustenance, maintenance, mercy, life, peace, and everything good; and of all good things may He never deprive us.

The compassionate One. May He reign over us forever. The compassionate One. May He be blessed on heaven and on earth. The compassionate One. May He be praised for all generations, may He be glorified through us to all eternity, and be honored through us forever and ever. The compassionate One. May He sustain us in honor. The compassionate One. May He break the yoke of oppression from our necks and guide us upright to our Land. The compassionate One. May He send us abundant blessing to this house and upon this table at which we have eaten. The compassionate One. May He send us Elijah, the Prophet, who is remembered for good, to proclaim to us good tidings, salvations, and consolations. The compassionate One. May He bless —

Children at their parents' home add the words in parentheses:
(my father, my teacher) the master of this house,
and (my mother, my teacher) lady of this house,

Those eating at their own home recite the following, adding the appropriate words in parentheses:
me (my wife/husband and family) and all that is mine,

Guests recite the following:
them, their house, their family, and all that is theirs,

all continue here:
ours and all that is ours — just as our forefathers Abraham, Isaac, and Jacob were blessed in everything, from everything, with everything. So may He bless us all together with a perfect blessing. And let us say: Amen.

On high, may merit be invoked upon them and upon us, for the merit of peace. May we receive a blessing from Hashem and kindness from the God of our deliverance, and find favor and understanding in the eyes of God and man.

On Shabbat add the following sentence:
The compassionate One. May He allow us inherit the day which will be completely Shabbat, and rest for eternal life.
The words in parentheses are added on the two Seder nights:
The compassionate One. May He cause us to inherit that day which is totally good, (that eternal day, the day when the just will sit with crowns on their heads, enjoying their proximity to God — and may our portion be with them)

The compassionate One. May He make us worthy to experience the days of Messiah and the life of the World to Come. He Who is a tower of salvations to His King and shows loving-kindness to his anointed, to David and his descendants forever. He Who makes peace in His heavenly heights, may He make peace for us and for all Israel. Say: Amen.

Fear Hashem, His holy ones, for those who fear Him are not aware of deprivation. Young lions may feel want and hunger, but those who seek Hashem will not lack any good. Give thanks to God for He is good; His loving-kindness is eternal. You open Your hand and satisfy the desire of every living being. Blessed is the man who trusts in Hashem, and Hashem will be his trust. I was a youth and also have aged, and I have not seen a righteous man forsaken, with his children begging for bread. Hashem will give strength to His nation; Hashem will bless His nation with peace.

STOP *The following blessing is said before drinking the third cup of wine. One should try to finish the entire cup, or at least, most of it. Again, we are careful to lean to the left while drinking.*

Blessed are You, Hashem, our God, King of the universe, Who creates the fruit of the vine.

בָּרוּךְ אַתָּה יהוה אֱלֹהֵינוּ מֶלֶךְ הָעוֹלָם בּוֹרֵא פְּרִי הַגָּפֶן:

Baruch attah Adonai, eloheynu melech ha-olam, boray p'ri ha-gafen.

STOP *The fourth cup of wine is now poured. Also, the cup of Elijah, (Eliyahu the Prophet) is poured at this point.*

The front door to the house is now opened. This is in keeping with the idea that the night of Passover is considered laiyl shimurim, 'a night of guarded protection'. With the door open, the following paragraph is recited.

Pour Your anger upon the nations that do not pay attention to You; and upon the kingdom that do not take Your Name into consideration. They have devoured Jacob and destroyed His Habitation. Pour Your anger upon them, and let Your wrath finally catch-up to them. Pursue them with wrath and annihilate them from beneath the heavens of Hashem.

HALLEL (PRAISE)

STOP *After closing the door everyone recites the Hallel-Praises. These should be read at a comfortable pace.*

Hallel

Not for our sake, O God, not for our sake, but for Your Name's sake give honor, for the sake of Your loving-kindness and Your truth. Why should the nations say: 'Where is their God?' Our God is in the heavens; everything is according to His will. Their idols are silver and gold, the work of human hands. They have a mouth, but cannot speak; they have eyes, but cannot see; they have ears, but cannot hear; they have a nose, but cannot smell; their hands – cannot touch; their feet – cannot walk; nor can they utter a sound with their throat. Those who make them should become like them, whoever trusts in them. O Israel. Trust in Hashem — He is their help and shield. House of Aaron. Trust in Hashem. He is their help and shield. You who fear Hashem. Trust in Hashem, He is their help and shield.

Hashem Who has remembered us; will bless. He will bless the House of Israel; He will bless the House of Aaron; He will bless those who fear Hashem, the small and also the great. May Hashem add increase upon you, upon you and your children. You are blessed of Hashem, who makes the heaven and earth. The heaven: the heaven is Hashem's; but the earth: He has given to mankind. The dead cannot praise Hashem, nor any who go down in silence. But we will bless our God from this time forward, forever. Halleluyah.

I love when Hashem hears my voice, my prayers. For He has inclined His ear to me, throughout my days I will call upon Him. The pangs of death encompassed me; the narrow confines of the grave have caught-up with me; trouble and sorrow I have found. Then I called upon the Name of Hashem: 'Please Hashem, save my soul', Gracious is Hashem and righteous, our God is merciful. God protects the simple; I was brought low, and He saved me. Return my soul to your rest, for Hashem has greatly rewarded you. You freed my soul from death, my eyes from tears, and my foot from stumbling. I will walk before God in the lands of the living. I kept faith although I say: 'I suffer very much.' I said in my haste: 'All mankind is deceitful.'

How can I repay Hashem for all the rewards He has given me? I will raise the cup of deliverance, and call in the Name of Hashem. My vows to Hashem will I fulfill in the presence of his entire people. Precious in the eyes of Hashem is the death of His devoted ones. Please, Hashem, for I am Your servant, I am Your servant, son of Your handmaid. You have released my bonds. To You I sacrifice thanksgiving offerings, and the Name of Hashem will I invoke. My vows to Hashem will I fulfill in the presence of His entire people; in the courtyards of the House of Hashem, in your midst, Jerusalem. Halleluyah.

Praise Hashem, all you nations; praise Him, all you peoples. For His kindness to us was overwhelming, us, and the truth of Hashem is eternal. Halleluyah.

Give thanks to Hashem for he is good; His kindness is eternal.

Let Israel say: His kindness is eternal.

Let the House of Aaron say: His kindness is eternal.

Let them who fear Hashem say: His kindness is eternal.

From out of the straits I called to God; God answered me with a feeling of expansiveness. Hashem is with me, and so I do not fear; what can man do to me? Hashem is with me, to help me; therefore I can face my enemies. It is better to rely on Hashem than to rely on princes. All nations surround me; but in the Name of Hashem I cut them down. They surround me. They surrounded me from all sides; but in the Name of Hashem, I cut them down. They surround me like bees, but they are extinguished like the thorns by fire; in the Name of Hashem I cut them down. You have continuously pushed me that I might fall, but Hashem assisted me. My strength and song is God; He has become my salvation. The sound of rejoicing and salvation is in the tents of the righteous: 'The right hand of Hashem does valiantly.. The right hand of Hashem is raised triumphantly. The right hand of Hashem is exalted. I shall not die. I shall live and relate the deeds of God. God has chastised me exceedingly, but He did not let me die. Open for me the gates of righteousness, I will enter them and be thankful to God. This is the gate of Hashem; the righteous shall enter through it. I thank You for You answered me and became my deliverance. I thank You for You answered me and became my deliverance. The very stone which the builders despised has become the cornerstone. The very stone which the builders despised has become the cornerstone. This was done by Hashem; it is wondrous in our eyes. This was done by Hashem; it is wondrous in our eyes. This is the day Hashem has made; we will rejoice and be happy in Him. This is the day Hashem has made; we will rejoice and be happy in Him.

Hashem, please save us.

Hashem, please save us.

Hashem, please make us prosper.

Hashem, please make us prosper.

Blessed is the one who comes in the Name of Hashem; we bless you from the House of Hashem. Blessed is the one who comes in the Name of Hashem; we bless you from the House of Hashem. Hashem is God and has illuminated for us; bind the festival offering with cords to the corners of the altar. Hashem is God and has illuminated for us; bind the festival offering with cords to the corners of the altar. You are my God and I will thank You; my God, I will exalt You. You are my God and I will thank you, my God, I will exalt You. Be grateful to Hashem, for He is good; His kindness is eternal. Be grateful to Hashem, for He is good; His kindness is eternal.

They will praise You, Hashem our God for all of Your deeds, along with Your devoted followers, the righteous, who do Your will, and Your entire nation, the House of Israel, joyfully thank you, bless, praise, laud, exalt, revere, sanctify, and crown Your name, our King. For to You it is proper to give thanks, and to Your name it is appropriate to sing praises, for from eternity and to eternity You are God. Blessed are You God, the One who is most praiseworthy.

Give thanks to Hashem, for He is good;	His kindness is eternal.
Give thanks to the God of gods;	His kindness is eternal.
Give thanks to the Master of masters;	His kindness is eternal.
To the only one who does great wonders;	His kindness is eternal.
To He who fashioned the cosmos with understanding	His kindness is eternal.
To He Who placed the earth over the waters;	His kindness is eternal.
To He Who made the great celestial lights;	His kindness is eternal.
The sun to reign during day;	His kindness is eternal.
The moon and the stars to reign at night	His kindness is eternal.
To He Who struck the Egyptians through their firstborn;	
	His kindness is eternal.
And removed Israel from amongst them;	His kindness is eternal.
With a strong hand and an outstretched arm;	His kindness is eternal.
He Who divided the Sea into parts;	His kindness is eternal.

And caused Israel to pass through it;   His kindness is eternal.
And threw Pharaoh and his army into the Sea of Reeds;
                                                                                His kindness is eternal.
To He Who led His people through the wilderness;   His kindness is eternal.
To He Who destroyed great kings;   His kindness is eternal.
And slew mighty kings;   His kindness is eternal.
Sichon, king of Emorites;   His kindness is eternal.
And Og, king of Bashan;   His kindness is eternal.
And gave their land as an inheritance   His kindness is eternal.
An inheritance of Israel. His servant: His kindness is eternal.
He Who remembered us at our lowest moment;   His kindness is eternal.
And released us from our enemies;   His kindness is eternal.
He gives food to all living creatures;   His kindness is eternal.
Be thankful to God of heaven;   His kindness is eternal.

The soul of every living being will bless Your Name, Hashem our God; All spirited flesh will continuously glorify and exalt Your remembrance, our King. From eternity to eternity, You are God, and besides You we have no king, redeemer or helper. O Rescuer, Redeemer, Sustainer and Merciful One in all times of desperation and distress. We have no King but You – God of the first and of the last, God of all creatures, Master of all generations, Who is extolled through numerous praises, He Who guides His world with kindness and His creatures with compassion Hashem does not slumber or sleep; He rouses the sleepers and awakens the ones who slumber; He makes the mute speak and frees those who are imprisoned; He supports the ones who are falling and raises erect the bowed down. Only to you do we give thanks.

If our mouths were as full of song as the sea, and our tongue as full of rejoicing as its many waves, and our lips as full of praise as the expanse of the heavens, and our eyes as brilliant as the sun and the moon, and our hands as outspread in prayer as the eagles of the sky and our feet as swift as deer: Still we could not thank You enough. Hashem our God and God of our fathers, bless Your Name, for each one of the thousands and thousands and myriads upon myriads of kindness, miracles and wonders, which You performed for our fathers, and for us. You liberated us from Egypt. Hashem our God, and took us out of the house of bondage. In famine You nourished us, and in plenty You were the source of our support. You saved us from the sword; from the plague You let us escape; and You spared us from severe and enduring diseases. Until now Your compassion has helped us, and Your kindness has never left us. Do not abandon us, Hashem our God – ever.

The limbs which You set within us, and the spirit and soul which You breathed into our nostrils, and the tongue which You put in our mouth – they must all thank and bless, praise and glorify, exalt, be devoted to, sanctify and honor Your Name, our King, forever. Every mouth must give thanks to You, every tongue must vow allegiance to You; every knees must bend to You; all who stand must bow before You; all hearts must fear You; and men's innermost feelings and thoughts will certainly singe praises to Your name, as it is written; All my bones will say: 'Hashem, who is like You?' You save the poor man from the one who is stronger than him, the impoverished and the needy from one who would try to rob him. Who can be compared to You? Who is equal to You? Who can be compared to You? Great, powerful, and awesome God, supreme God, Maker of heaven and earth. We shall praise, extol, and glorify You; and bless Your holy Name, as it says; A Psalm of David: Bless Hashem, my soul, and let my whole being bless His holy name.

God, in the omnipotence of Your strength, great is the honor of Your name, externally powerful and awesome through Your wondrous deeds, King who is enthroned on a high and lofty throne.

He Who abides externally, exalted and holy is His Name. And it is written Be joyful in Hashem, you righteous ones; for the upright, His praise is fitting. By the mouth of the upright You will be praised; by the words of the righteous You will be blessed; by the tongue of the devoted You will be exalted; and amongst the holy You will be sanctified.

And in the assemblies of Your countless people, the House of Israel, with excitement will Your name, our King, be glorified in every generation. For such the responsibility of all creatures; before You, Hashem, our God and God of our fathers, to thank, praise, laud, glorify, extol, adore, bless, exalt, and sing praises; even beyond all expressions of the songs and praises of David the son of Jesse, Your servant, Your anointed one.

May Your Name be praised forever, our King, the God and King Who is great and holy in heaven and on earth; for to You, Hashem our God and God of our fathers, it is most fitting to sing song and praise, hallel and hymns, strength and sovereignty, victory, greatness and power, praise and glory, holiness and sovereignty, blessing and thanks, from now and forever. Blessed are You, Hashem, God, King, who is praised greatly, God of thanksgiving, Master of wonders, Who favors songs of praise – King, God, Life of all worlds.

STOP *At the conclusion of Hallel, the fourth cup of wine is drunk. One should finish all or most of the cup. As with the other cups, one leans to the left while drinking. The following blessing is said before one begins to drink.*

Blessed are You, Hashem, our God, King of the universe, Who creates the fruit of the vine.

בָּרוּךְ אַתָּה יהוה אֱלֹהֵינוּ מֶלֶךְ הָעוֹלָם בּוֹרֵא פְּרִי הַגָּפֶן:

Baruch attah Adonai, eloheynu melech ha-olam, boray p'ri ha-gafen.

STOP *The following blessing is recited after drinking the fourth cup. The phrases in parentheses are added on Shabbat.*

Blessed are You, Hashem, our God, King of the universe, for the vine and the fruit of the vine; and for the produce of the field; for the lovely, good, and spacious land which You graciously gave our forefathers as an inheritance; to eat its fruit and be filled by its goodness. Please have compassion, Hashem, our G-d on Israel Your nation, on Jerusalem Your city, and on Zion where Your honor dwells; and on Your altar and on Your Temple. May You rebuild Jerusalem, Your holy city, quickly in our days; and take us up to it and let us rejoice in its rebuilding, and let us eat from its fruit and be filled with its goodness: and bless You in a state of sanctity and purity. (Find favor with us and give us strength on this Shabbat day.) And let us be happy on this festival of matzahs. You, Hashem, are good and benevolent to all creatures, and we give thanks to You for the land and the fruit of the vine. Blessed are You, Hashem, for the land and the fruit of the vine.

NIRTZAH

STOP *The following prayer is read by everyone.*

The Seder is now concluded in accordance with it's laws; Its ordinances, and its statutes. Just as we have been privileged to experience it, so may we merit to perform it. O Pure One, Who dwells on high, raise up the countless congregation; and soon — please guide the offshoots of Your plants, redeemed, to Zion with joyous songs.

L'SHANA HABAH B'YERUSHOLAYIM — NEXT YEAR IN JERUSALEM!

9

EPILOGUE

*S*teve wears a warm smile and sports stylish suspenders. His spry, robust gate and affable congeniality belie a fierce dedication to his task as teacher, counselor, friend, and jack-of-all-trades. Music was the passion of his youth. As an undergrad, he followed his heart towards music and social work. It was Segovia and Skinner, not Akiva and Hillel, who then occupied his mind.

Eventually Steve became Rabbi Steve. For years he served as the Hillel director on a campus with a Jewish population of four thousand in a student body of nearly sixty thousand. Come Passover, Rabbi Steve poured his heart into creating a meaningful Seder experience for his students. With over two hundred students present, the annual Hillel Seder was a well-attended Jewish event.

One year a young man named Mitchell registered for the Seder. His name was not a familiar one and Rabbi Steve looked forward to meeting him.

Not long after the Seder began, the rabbi felt a tap on his shoulder. In a perplexed and whispery voice, Mitchell asked, "What's going on here, and by the way, what are those books that everyone has been given?"

"This," Rabbi Steve began to patiently explain, "is a Seder, and that book is a Haggadah. It is..." But before he could finish, Mitchell's voice broke in: "But where is the food?" And while the rabbi assured him that food would be coming, all his eloquent efforts at interesting Mitchell in joining the Seder were to no avail. Mitchell already had plans for the evening. He had expected a Seder like the one back home — a family dinner with matzah — not something that seemed more like Temple than anything else. With that, Mitchell excused himself and left. And Rabbi Steve never saw him again.

Throughout the Haggadah portion of this book, questions were posed by three children. One simple, one wise, and one rebellious. Though the Haggadah speaks of a fourth child, in this book he never once asks a question. That was Mitchell — *the son who had other plans.*

In many ways this book was written for Mitchell. Wherever he is today, I hope that some circuitous course of events lands this book right in his lap. Amused by its looks, I hope he opens it up and begins to read. Further, I hope he shows it to his sister. Having discussed it, I hope they decide to reinstate a family gathering at Passover. Through the experience of that Seder I hope that they, and those who join them, will gain an inkling of what Passover is, or can be, all about.

If you are Mitchell — or his sister, mother, brother, father, wife, son, daughter, aunt, uncle, cousin, friend, or neighbor — then I hope this book has been a source of inspiration. I hope that you will walk away from this year's Seder seeing Judaism as an authentic medium through which you can thoughtfully examine the events of your inner life, as well as your Jewish life. That you will be motivated to accept the challenge of freedom with fresh determination and courage. And, if you have so benefited, I would ask you once again — please — share our legacy with someone you love.

As the great sage Hillel said:

If I am not for myself, who will be for me?
the adventure of growth is ours
And if I am only for myself, then what am I?
her fruits are ours to share
And if not now, when?

LE VIATHAN PRESS

AVAILABLE NOW:

Rosh Hashanah Yom Kippur Survival Kit
by Shimon Apisdorf   1993 Benjamin Franklin Award

Passover Survival Kit

Survival Kit Haggadah

FORTHCOMING PUBLICATIONS:

Missiles, Masks and Miracles
by Sam Veffer
*Morning-after interviews with residents of Tel Aviv apartments
destroyed by Scud missiles during the Gulf War. Gripping personal
stories.*

Love and Marriage Survival Kit

Chanukah Revival Kit
*Chanukah is transformed into a source of spirituality, self-growth
and inner lights.*

HOW TO ORDER

Retail Sales: Call 1-800-583-2476 or 1-800-860-0774

Leviathan Books – Gifts to Grow With!
We will gladly include personalized holiday and
greeting cards at no extra cost.
Call 1-800-583-2476 for more information.

Group Sales: Synagogues, schools and community organizations have ordered over 25,000 copies of our books for fundraising,   PR and educational purposes. We have innovative programs for your group to make the best use of these unique publications. Significant special-order discounts available.

Call us at **1-800-860-0774** or write:

Leviathan Press Marketing
66 North Merkle Road
P.O.Box 43209-0448
Columbus, Ohio 43209

ABOUT THE AUTHOR

Shimon Apisdorf is an ordained Rabbi who studied at the University of Cincinnati, Telshe Yeshiva of Cleveland and Yeshivat Aish HaTorah in Jerusalem. Originally from Cleveland, he enjoys taking long walks with his wife, feeding the ducks with his children and going to football games with his father. His first book, the Rosh Hashanah Yom Kippur Survival Kit, was recognized by the Publishers Marketing Association with a Benjamin Franklin Award, and has been hailed as a ground-breaking work. These books speak clearly to a generation grappling with the issues of spirituality, self-awareness and growth. Through his writings and talks one is invited to explore the down-to-earth relevance of Jewish thought in the contemporary world. For speaking engagements call, 1-800-860-0774.

ABOUT THE COVER

Our cover illustration was painted by the renowned Canadian illustrator Julius Ciss. For almost two decades Julius has been an institution in Canadian illustration. Julius' sensitivity to human nature, keen eye for detail and refreshing sense of humor are the trademarks of his acrylic paintings that

capture precious moments in Jewish life.

For information on how to obtain limited edition prints of cover paintings in the Survival Kit series of books contact;

Julius Ciss Illustration Inc.,
P.O. Box 54582
1712 Avenue Road
Toronto, Ontario
Canada M5M4N5
(416) 784-1416